First edition published in the UK 2006 by Mallams Publishing Ltd.
This updated edition published by The Book Business, 2009
www.thebookbiz.com

Text copyright © 2009 Christine Smeeth & Kathy Sharp
Front Cover and Illustrations © Al Smeeth 2009
Photographs: Christine Smeeth / Kathy Sharp
The right of Christine Smeeth & Kathy Sharp to be identified as the authors
of this work has been asserted by them in accordance with the Copyright,
Designs and Patents Act, 1988.

A Cataloguing-in-Publication Data catalogue record for this title is available
from the British Library

ISBN: 978-1-905412-24-2

**Printed by Quay Digital, Portishead
www.quaydigital.net**

Papers used by The Book Business are natural, recyclable products made from
wood grown in sustainable forests. The manufacturing processes conform to the
environmental regulations of the country of origin.

Garden Plants that Slugs Won't Eat!

Christine Smeeth

Kathy Sharp

**In memory of our
shared garden.**

Contents

The Culprits in the Garden

Slugs will eat worms and other dead slugs.

An average garden contains approximately 200 slugs and snails.

Slugs and snails prefer to hide in dark, damp places.

Snails are hermaphrodite, as are slugs. They can function as both male or female and a union can result in the production of offspring.

Introduction

Slug and snail attacks, often carried out by stealth in the dead of night, are the cause of many a garden disappointment. It's no fun at all to step outside on a pleasant spring morning only to find the gloopy tell-tale silvery trails among the munched remains of your precious plants.

Many people prefer not to use chemicals in the garden these days. This may be because you have pets or children using the garden, or you may wish to garden organically or encourage wildlife. You may find yourself attempting to choose between expensive, messy or downright ineffective means of slug control, while the horrid creatures continue to devastate your plants.

Why Slugs and Snails are so Successful

Snails and, especially, slugs may appear to be the lowliest of creatures, but they are very well-adapted to making an excellent living from our gardens. So what is it about their habits and life-cycles that makes them so successful?

Double Trouble....

To begin with slugs and snails are hermaphrodites (that is, both sexes at once). This means that following a romantic encounter, both the little blighters go off to lay eggs. This is obviously a very quick way of increasing the population, and goes some way to explaining why there are so many of them. Gardeners assist the process by providing plenty of nooks and crannies for them to lay eggs in - pot rims, walls, fences and lots of freshly-dug bare soil.

Lots to Eat....

You may be alarmed to hear that, with luck, a well-nourished snail can survive for quite a few years. Between them, slugs and snails will eat a wide range of plant matter, both fresh and decayed, above ground and below. Our gardens provide them with everything they need for a full and jolly life, from succulent seedlings to delicious bedding plants, fresh from the garden centre, to any number of bits of plant debris that will do just as well. Snails, at least, have the good grace to hibernate during the winter, but slugs can carry on munching on any mild winter day, so the devastation can continue round the year.

A place to Live...

Yes, we provide that, too. Slugs, always in danger of drying out, need a cool place to lurk in hot weather. Under the shed, beneath a paving slab, some nice shady foliage or in the soil itself will do nicely. Snails can plug themselves shut to prevent heat loss, but they like a nice safe place to take their siesta, halfway up an evergreen shrub being their favourite.

Before you rush to blame the slugs and snails...

Bear in mind that slugs and snails will feed on most kinds of decaying matter. If your plant has died for other reasons, slugs may still be attracted to the dying plant.

Although slugs and snails normally do not eat the foliage of daffodils, for instance, they may well help themselves to the remains of the leaves as they die down. This is not really a slug or snail attack – the leaves will die anyway. The slugs are just clearing up the debris.

Any plant put in a situation where the soil or amount of sun or dampness do not suit it will be weakened, as will one that is not watered and cared for properly when it is newly-planted. A weak plant, even of a normally resistant type, may be prone to attack, so we can't make any absolute guarantees. However we can point you in the direction of a big choice of plants that stand a fighting chance - and warn you about the most susceptible types.

Slug and Snail Resistant Plants - a new approach to an old problem

If you choose your plants carefully, slug and snail damage can be reduced to a minimum, or even prevented altogether.

Whether you are starting from scratch with a new garden, renovating an existing one, or simply deciding what annuals and bedding plants to get this year, this book will help you make informed choices and avoid disappointments.

Slug & Snail Resistant Plants

You will soon see that there is a huge range of plants that slugs and snails show little interest in.

Shrubs are rarely attacked by either slugs or snails, and neither are grasses, rushes, sedges or ferns. Among herbaceous plants, those with aromatic, grey or hairy leaves are generally more resistant to attack.

We cannot guarantee that no slug will ever set its rasping mouthparts to your plants again, but we hope it will become less troublesome.

So before you make any further plans for your garden, or buy any more plants from the garden centre, check the information in this book. You can look at our suggestions for plants to use in specific situations in the garden, or for specific purposes, or go straight to our Directory of Plants (*See page 25*) and check our resistance or susceptibility rating for any commonly available garden plant.

We have added a 'See at a Glance' Guide to make life easier.

Key: These plants are not usually attacked.

 May be attacked.

 Very susceptible to slugs and snails.

Facts about Slugs

By hoeing regularly the slugs and eggs cannot hide easily in the top soil of the garden. Many creatures feast on slugs and their eggs, which is a good reason to bring them to the surface, including birds, moles, hedgehogs, some beetles, frogs, and millipedes.

Slugs hide in overhanging shrubs and lawn edgings. Sharp grit sprinkled over the top of plants helps to keep them off young shoots.

Slugs hide in overhanging shrubs and lawn edgings. Sharp grit sprinkled over the top of plants helps to keep them off young shoots.

Each slug can produce up to 36 eggs, several times a year. Which is a lot of reproduction. The white-jelly eggs are laid underground and hatch within 10-21 days. Baby slugs reach adulthood (munching all the way) in approximately six weeks.

Each season a slug can eat up to 1¾ lb of plants.

Popular Anti-Slug & Snail Remedies, and what's wrong with them

Anti-slug remedies fall into four basic groups:

killing the slugs directly or indirectly;
luring them away from susceptible plants;
putting down barriers they won't cross;
cultural remedies

Slug & Snail Killers

Natural Predators. The ideal solution. A wildlife pond full of frogs and toads is one of the most successful permanent solutions to the slug problem, as these creatures will eat them. However, ponds can be quite expensive to install, and require a good deal of maintenance. And if you have small children they can, of course, be dangerous. Other wildlife, including hedgehogs will eat slugs, but unless you have a wild garden it may not be easy to attract them.

Nematodes. These slug parasites are another quite successful means of control. You water them into the soil around susceptible plants. The disadvantages are that they are expensive, and the effect will only last a few weeks, or less if the weather is wet.

Torchlight Ambush. This involves becoming the predator yourself and going out after dark and picking the slugs off your plants and disposing of them. It's a very organic solution, and cost-free. But it's very time-consuming; and how exactly do you dispose of the slugs? There's no pleasant answer to this question. A popular method is to drown them in a bucket of salty water and add the resulting sludge to your compost. Not for the squeamish.

Slug Pellets. The traditional answer, and it certainly kills them. You will find dozens of dead slugs around the pellets in a vast mass of congealed slime. Yuk! Expensive, messy and unsuitable for children, pets, organic or wildlife gardens. Some more 'organic' pellets are now available and said to be less toxic, but they still involve putting expensive chemicals all over your garden.

Lures

Bran. This is one of many popular slug baits. The slugs eat it, it expands inside them, and ultimately they explode. This is certainly an organic, non-chemical solution which poses no great danger to children or pets. But do you really want a garden full of exploded slugs? There is also the danger, in common with other baits, that some other undesirable forms of wildlife might be attracted, such as rats.

Beer Traps. Slugs enjoy beer, and can be lured into a trap containing it, where they will at least die happy. However, lots of other creatures, many of them useful to the gardener, also enjoy beer and fall into the traps. The traps must be cleared and topped up frequently, which makes this quite a time-consuming remedy, not to mention the cost of the beer.

Other Baits. These usually consist of items such as potato or cabbage peelings or grapefruit skins. The theory is that the slugs are lured away from your plants, and you can then collect them up. It's certainly an organic approach. but this method has the disadvantage of being messy and time-consuming. You have a garden full of food rubbish, which may attract other undesirable animals,and you still have to get rid of the slugs and snails at the end of the day. And don't forget the slugs you *don't* manage to catch; they will be well-fed and raring to breed.

Planks, Bricks and Old Sacks. This is the daylight version of Torchlight Ambush, above. You leave a selection of cool, shady hiding places around the garden, such as a piece of old carpet, which will attract the slugs and snails to shelter under during the day and collect them up at your leisure. If you don't mind all this junk lurking in your garden then it's a cheap organic solution.

Putting down Barriers

Mulches. These vary in their effectiveness and in their cost. Some kinds of composted bark may help to deter slugs, but this is an expensive route to take. Gravels are often recommended, but we have found they are not particularly effective, especially in wet weather.

Copper Bands. We have found these to be an expensive and not particularly effective solution.

Vaseline. This can be quite effective round the rim of a pot, but we have heard of people picking pots up to move them, and having them slip through their fingers and breaking. And it's no use at all for plants growing directly in the ground, of course.

Other barriers. There is quite a selection of materials used as barriers which slugs are reluctant to cross. These include salt, coffee grounds, soot, builders' plaster and wood ash. Some of these are actually harmful to plants as well as slugs. If you don't mind these unpleasant substances all over your garden, by all means try them. But in general it's not good for the soil and it's certainly not very organic.

Cultural Remedies

Garden Hygiene. The theory is that if you clear up all debris and garden rubbish and keep everything clean and tidy the slugs and snails will have fewer places to hide and breed. If you have the time and inclination for this kind of pernickety gardening, it may well help, slug-wise, but it will also discourage other, more useful, forms of wildlife.

Regular Hoeing. Keeping weed cover to a minimum by hoeing between plants allows the soil to dry out more and provides fewer places for slugs to lurk. Or so they say. This is clearly a cost-free but time-consuming approach, and unhelpful if you want your plants to self-seed around the garden.

Garden Plants that Slugs Won't Eat!

200 Plants, Vegetables and Fruit that Slugs won't eat!

Quick Reference List

Well, more than two hundred in fact. They are all reasonably slug and snail resistant, although a few might get a little chewed initially they quickly revive as the plant gets stronger. The selection includes shrubs, herbaceous perennials, bulbs, corms annuals and biennials. For further information see the Directory of Plants, (*See page 25*).

Abelia
Abutilon
Acanthus (Bear's Breeches)
Achillea (Yarrow)
Aconitum (Monkshood)
Acorus
Actinidia
Adiantum (Maidenhair Fern)
Aeonium
Ajuga (Bugle)
Alchemilla (Lady's Mantle)
Allium (Garlic)
Anaphalis (Pearly Everlasting)
Androsace (Rock Jasmine)
Anemone hupehensis (Japanese Anemone)
Anemone x hybrida (Japanese Anemone)
Anthemis (Camomile)
Anthriscus (Cow Parsley; Chervil)
Antirrhinum (Snapdragon)
Apples (although they are partial to windfalls)
Aquilegia (Columbine)
Arabis (Rockcress)
Arisaema
Arisarum (Mouse Plant)
Armeria (Thrift)
Artemisia (Wormwood)
Aruncus (Goat's Beard)
Asplenium (Spleenwort)

> Some gardeners chop slugs in half or stamp on them. Effective, but not for the squemish!

Garden Plants that Slugs Won't Eat!

Aster amellus
Aster x *frikartii*
Aster novae-angliae (Michaelmas Daisy)
Astilbe (Goat's Beard)
Astrantia (Masterwort)
Athyrium (Lady Fern)
Aucuba (Spotted Laurel)
Aurinia (Yellow Alyssum)
Ballota
Bamboos
Baptisia (Wild Indigo)
Bassia (*Kochia*; Burning Bush)
Beetroot
Begonia
Bellis (Daisy)
Berberis
Bergenia (Elephant's Ears)
Billardiera
Blackberry
Blackcurrant
Blechnum
Bletilla (Garden Orchid)
Borago (Borage)
Brachyglottis
Brachyscome (Swan River Daisy)
Briza (Quaking Grass)
Brunnera
Buddleja (Butterfly Bush)
Buxus (Box)

Calamagrostis (Feather Reed Grass)
Calamintha (Calamint)
Calendula (Pot Marigold)
Callistemon (Bottlebrush)
Callistephus (China Aster)
Calluna (Ling; Heather)
Caltha (Marsh Marigold)
Camassia (Quamash)
Camellia
Campanula poscharskyana (Serbian Bellflower)
Campsis (Trumpet Vine)
Canna (Indian Shot)

Carex (Sedge)
Caryopteris (Blue Spiraea)
Catananche (Cupid's Dart)
Cauliflower
Ceanothus (Californian Lilac)
Celery
Celastrus (Bittersweet)
Centaurea dealbata
Centaurea montana (Perennial Cornflower)
Cephalaria
Cerastium (Snow-in-Summer)
Ceratostigma
Chaenomeles (Quince)
Chamaemelum (Camomile)
Chelone (Turtlehead)
Chimonobambusa
Chionochloa (Tussock Grass)
Chionodoxa (Glory of the Snows)
Choisya (Mexican Orange Blossom)
Chrysanthemum
Chusquea
Cimicifuga
Cistus (Rock rose)
Clarkia (*Godetia*)
Clematis
Cobaea (Cup and Saucer Vine)
Cordyline (Cabbage Palm)
Coriandrum (Coriander)
Cortaderia (Pampas Grass)
Corydalis lutea
Cotoneaster
Crinum
Crocosmia (Montbretia)
Crocus
Cyclamen
Cynara (Cardoon)
Cytisus (Broom)
Cyrtonium (Holly Fern)
Daboecia
Daphne
Davallia (Squirrel's Foot Fern)

Garden Plants that Slugs Won't Eat!

Deschampsia (Hair Grass)
Dianthus, except *D. barbatus* (Sweet William)
Diascia
Dicksonia (Tree Fern)
Dierama (Angel's Fishing Rods)
Digitalis (Foxglove)
Doronicum (Leopard's Bane)
Dracunculus (Dragon Arum)
Dryopteris (Buckler Fern)
Echeveria
Echinops (Globe Thistle)
Echium
Eccremocarpus (Chilean Glory Vine)
Elaeagnus
Elymus (Elytrigia)
Eranthis (Winter Aconite)
Eremurus (Foxtail Lily)
Erica (Heath)
Erigeron (Fleabane)
Erinus (Fairy Foxglove)
Erodium (Storksbill)
Eryngium (Sea Holly)
Escallonia
Eschscholzia (Californian Poppy)
Eucomis (Pineapple Lily)
Euonymus (Spindle)
Eupatorium
Euphorbia (Spurge)
Euryops
Exochorda
Fallopia (Mile-a-Minute Plant)
Fargesia
Felicia
Ferns
Festuca (Fescue)
Filipendula (Meadowsweet)
Foeniculum (Fennel)
Forsythia
Fothergilla
Francoa
Fuchsia

Unless you grow the peppery type of salad leaves you will need to use slug traps. Salad leaves develop a bitter taste if the soil is moist and slugs and snails adore moist and damp!

Gaillardia (Blanket Flower)
Galanthus (Snowdrop)
Galega (Goat's Rue)
Galium odoratum (Woodruff)
Galtonia (Summer Hyacinth)
Gaultheria
Gaura
Gazania (Treasure Flower)
Genista
Geranium (Cranesbill)
Geum (Avens)
Glyceria (Reed Grass)
Griselinia
Gunnera
Gypsophila (annuals only)
Hakonochloa (Hakone Grass)
Halimium
Hebe
Hedera (Ivy)
Hedychium (Ginger Lily)

Helianthemum (Rockrose)
Helichrysum
Helictotrichon (Oat Grass)
Heliopsis
Heliotropium (Cherry Pie)
Hesperis (Dame's Violet; Sweet Rocket)
Heuchera (Coral Bells)
X *Hibanobambusa*
Himalayacalamus
Holcus (Velvet Grass)
Hordeum (Barley)
Houttuynia
Humulus (Hop)
Hyacinthoides (Bluebell)
Hydrangea
Hypericum (St John's Wort)
Iberis sempervirens (Perennial Candytuft)
Impatiens (Busy Lizzie)
Imperata (Blood Grass)
Indocalamus
Inula

Garden Plants that Slugs Won't Eat!

Jasminum (Jasmine)
Jovibarba (Hen and Chickens Houseleek)
Juncus (Rushes)
Kalmia
Kerria
Knautia (Scabious)
Lagurus (Hare's Tail Grass)
Lamium (Deadnettle)
Lantana
Laurentia
Laurus (Bay)
Lavandula (Lavender)
Lavatera (Tree Mallow)
Leucanthemum (Oxeye and Shasta Daisies)
Leucojum (Snowflake)
Levisticum (Lovage)
Lewisia
Leycesteria (Pheasant Berry)
Libertia
Ligustrum (Privet)
Lilium regale only
Limnanthes (Poached Egg Plant)
Limonium (Statice; Sea Lavender)
Linaria (Toadflax)
Linum (Flax)
Lithodora
Lobularia (Alyssum; Sweet Alison)
Lonicera (Honeysuckle)
Lotus
Luma (Myrtle)
Lunaria (Honesty)
Luzula (Woodrushes)
Lychnis coronaria (Rose Campion)
Lysichiton (Skunk Cabbage)
Lysimachia (Loosestrife)
Lythrum (Purple Loosestrife)
Maclea
Mahonia
Malcolmia (Virginia Stock)
Malva (Mallow)
Matteuccia (Ostrich Fern)

Matthiola (Stock)
Melianthus
Melica (Melick)
Melissa (Lemon Balm)
Mentha (Mint)
Milium (Wood Millet)
Mimulus (Musk; Monkey Flower)
Mirabilis (Marvel of Peru)
Miscanthus (Eulalia Grass)
Molinia (Moor Grass)
Monarda (Beregamot; Bee Balm)
Morina (Whorl Flower)
Musa (Banana Plant)
Muscari (Grape Hyacinth)
Myosotis (Forgetmenot)
Nemesia
Nepeta (Catmint)
Nicandra (Shoo Fly Plant)
Nigella (Love-in-a-Mist)
Oenothera (Evening Primrose)
Olearia (Daisy Bush)
Onoclea (Sensitive Fern)
Ophiopogon (Lily Turf)
Origanum (Marjoram)
Ornithogalum (Star of Bethlehem)
Osmanthus
Osmunda (Royal Fern)
Osteospermum (Cape Daisy)
Ozothamnus
Pachysandra
Paeonia (Peony)
Panicum
Papaver nudicaule (Iceland Poppy)
Papaver orientale (Oriental Poppy)
Parahebe
Parthenocissus (Virginia Creeper)
Passiflora (Passion Flower)
Pelargonium (scented-leaved varieties)
Pennisetum (Feather Grass)
Perovskia (Russian Sage)
Persicaria

Garden Plants that Slugs Won't Eat!

Petasites (Butterbur)
Phalaris (Reed Canary Grass)
Phegopteris
Philadelphus (Mock Orange)
Phillyrea
Phlomis (Jerusalem Sage)
Phlox paniculata
Phormium (New Zealand Flax)
Photinia
Phuopsis
Phygelius (Cape Fuchsia)
Phyllodoce
Phyllostachys
Physalis (Chinese Lantern; Cape Gooseberry)
Physostegia (Obedient Plant)
Phytolacca
Pieris
Pittosporum
Plectranthus
Pleioblastus
Plum
Polemonium (Jacob's Ladder)
Polygala (Milkwort)
Polygonatum (Solomon's Seal)
Polypodium (Polypody)
Polystichum (Shield Fern)
Portulaca (Sun Plant)
Potentilla (Cinquefoil)
Prostanthera
Prunella (Self-heal)
Pseudosasa
Pterocephalus
Pulsatilla (Pasque Flower)
Puschkinia
Pyracantha (Firethorn)
Ranunculus
Raoulia
Raspberries
Rhodiola (Roseroot)
Rhodochiton (Purple Bell Vine)
Rhodohypoxis

Ribes (Flowering Currant)
Rodgersia
Romneya (Tree Poppy)
Rosa (Rose)
Rosmarinus (Rosemary)
Rudbeckia (Coneflower)
Ruta (Rue)
Salvia x *suberba* (Sage)
Sanguisorba (Burnet)
Santolina (Cotton Lavender)
Saponaria ocymoides (Tumbling Ted)
Sarcococca (Christmas Box)
Sasa
Sasaella
Satureja (Savory)
Saxifraga x *urbium* (London Pride)
Saxifraga umbrosa
Scabiosa caucasica (Scabious)
Scaevola (Fan Flower)
Schizanthus (Poor Man's Orchid)
Schizophragma
Scilla (Squill)
Sedum (Stonecrop)
Semiarundinaria
Sempervivum (Houseleek)
Sesleria
Setaria (Foxtail Millet)
Shibataea
Shortia
Sidalcea (Prairie Mallow)
Silene (Campion; Catchfly)
Sisyrinchium (Pigroot)
Skimmia
Smilacina
Solanum
Solenostemon (Coleus)
Solidago (Golden Rod)
Sparaxis (Harlequin Flower)
Spartium (Spanish Broom)
Spiraea (Bridal Wreath)
Stachys byzantina (Lamb's Ears)

Garden Plants that Slugs Won't Eat!

Stachys macrantha
Stephanandra
Sternbergia
Stipa (Feather Grass)
Strobilanthes
Symphoricarpos (Snowberry)
Symphytum (Comfrey)
Tamarix (Tamarisk)
Tanacetum (Feverfew; Tansy)
Telekia
Tellima
Teucrium (Germander)
Thalictrum aquilegifolium (Meadow Rue)
Thamnocalamus
Thunbergia (Black-eyed Susan)
Thymus (Thyme)
Tiarella (Foam Flower)
Tigridia (Tiger Flower)
Trachelospermum
Tradescantia virginiana (Spiderwort)
Triteleia
Tritonia
Trollius (Globe Flower)
Tropaeolum (Nasturtium)
Uncinia (Red Hook Sedge)
Valeriana (Valerian)
Verbascum (Mullein)
Verbena (Vervain)
Veronica (Speedwell)
Viburnum
Vinca (Periwinkle)
Vines
Weigela
Wisteria
Woodwardia
Yucca
Yushania
Zantedeschia (Arum)
Zauschneria
Zinnia

> Metaldehyde, used as liquid or pellets, is the most used chemical to control slugs and snails. Care should be taken because of the risk to wild animals and pets, who may consume them.

Which plants are susceptible and which are not?

Consult this *Directory of Plants* before you buy anything else from the garden centre…

In this list we have covered a range of commonly-available garden plants and assessed them for their resistance to slug or snail attack. Some plants have proved problematic, with some gardeners saying they have no trouble at all and others saying slugs have demolished theirs. In these instances we have erred on the side of caution and pointed out that they do sometimes come under attack from the dreaded molluscs.

Names
We have listed the plants under both common and botanical names, so you can look them up using either. Bear in mind that common names can vary in different parts of the country, and may also be applied to more than one plant.

Out of the Frying Pan…
Some plants have a problem apart from being eaten by slugs. This may be susceptibility to disease, other pests, or a tendency to become seriously invasive. Where this is the case we have added a warning.

Key: These plants are not usually attacked.

 May be attacked.

 Very susceptible to slugs and snails.

A

 Abelia
The abelias are lovely, late-flowering evergreen shrubs.

 Abutilon
These plants are not usually attacked by slugs or snails.

Acanthus (Bear's Breeches)

 Tall, handsome and architectural, the commonly-available *Acanthus mollis* is recommended as a border plant. The flowerheads can be dried.

Achillea (Yarrow)

Aromatic leaves render these herbaceous plants less liable to slug attack than some. *Achillea filipendulina* and its cultivars, such as 'Cloth of Gold' are particularly resistant and make large, spectacular back-of-border plants. The flowerheads can be dried, and retain their colour well.

Aconitum (Monkshood)

The poisonous chemicals present in the leaves makes Monkshood very slug and snail resistant. Be aware that it is equally poisonous to people.These very handsome plants do better in partial shade.

Acorus

These waterside plants are not usually attacked by slugs or snails. Vigorous and easy to propagate in spring or autumn by cutting rhizomes in small pieces, and planting in muddy ground.

 ### Actinidia
A climbing plant.

 ### Adiantum (Maidenhair Fern)

Adonis (Pheasant's Eye)

 Pheasant's eye is not recommended, as slugs like to munch the flower-buds.

Ageratum

 May attract slugs early on but once established they can flourish, although constant vigilance is necessary.

Aeonium

Aeoniums are tender succulents, but will survive outdoors in mild areas.

African Daisy see *Arctotis*

African Lily see *Agapanthus*

African Marigold see *Tagetes*

Agapanthus (African Lily)
Modern hybrids and cultivars tend to be more resistant.

Ajuga (Bugle)
An unbeatable groundcover plant, and shade tolerant, too.

Alcea (Hollyhock)
The lower leaves can get fairly well bitten, but it doesn't ultimately seem to damage hollyhock plants, although they can look rather scruffy. Grow them where the lower half of the stem is hidden by other plants.

Alchemilla (Lady's Mantle)
The thick hair on the leaves makes these perennials unattractive to slugs and snails. An excellent groundcover and front-of-border plant.

Alkanet see *Anchusa*

Alyssum see *Lobularia*

Alyssum, Yellow see *Aurinia*

Allium (Garlic)
The strong-smelling chemicals in the leaves of the decorative garlics puts off both slugs and snails. The popular large-flowered *Allium cristophii* makes an excellent border plant, and slugs don't usually touch the kitchen-herb chives (*Allium schoenoprasum*). The little yellow-flowered *Allium moly* comes recommended, too.

Alstroemeria (Peruvian Lily)
The young spring shoots are very attractive to slugs and snails. Not recommended.

Amaryllis (Jersey Lily, Belladonna Lily)
Not to be confused with the large-flowered indoor bulbs *Hippeastrum*, also known and often sold as *Amaryllis.*

Amicia

Anacyclus (Mount Atlas Daisy).

Anagallis (Pimpernel)

Anaphalis (Pearly Everlasting)

The flowerheads of these slug-resistant plants are very longlasting and can be dried, which makes them popular with flower arrangers. Many varieties have the added bonus of being drought tolerant.

Anchusa (Bugloss, Alkanet)

Androsace (Rock Jasmine)
Spring-flowering rock plants which are quite drought-resistant, too.

Anemone

Slugs and snails love anemones – they seem to find them irresistible. However, the late-flowering Japanese anemones, *Anemone hupehensis* and *Anemone* x *hybrida* are resistant. Beware: the Japanese Anemones can be invasive.

Anemonopsis

Anethum (Dill)

unusually for a herb, dill can be susceptible to slug and snail attack. Aromatic and 3ft (1 m) tall with a single stem and feathery leaves. Resembles fennel, but is shorter and has a subtler, aniseed flavour.

Angel's Fishing Rod see *Dierama*

Angel's Trumpet see *Brugmansia*

Anthemis (Camomile)
These aromatic plants are not affected by slugs and snails.

Anthriscus (Cow Parsley, Chervil)

Cow parsley is best known for the popular dark-leaved cultivar 'Ravenswing'.

Anthyllis
Young anthyllis plants may be susceptible to attack.

Antirrhinum (Snapdragon)

These popular plants are not attacked by slugs or snails. They are available in a vast range of colours and sizes, including trailing varieties. Recommended.

Aquilegia (Columbine, Granny's Bonnets)
The foliage is sometimes attacked later in the season by pests – the lovely variegated-leaved varieties are particularly susceptible.

Arabis (Rockcress)

Arctotis (African Daisy)

Arisaema

Arisarum (Mouse Plant)
The curious-looking plant *Arisarum* is not attacked by slugs or snails.

Armeria (Thrift)
All the thrifts have excellent evergreen foliage.

Artemisia (Wormwood)
The wormwoods are not attractive to slugs, including the lovely silver-leaved 'Powis Castle', and neither is the herb Tarragon. They make wonderful foliage plants and are perfect for an all-white border. As a bonus, they are also generally drought resistant.

Arum see *Zantedeschia*

Aruncus (Goat's Beard)
The goat's beards prefer a moist site.

Asarina (Creeping Snapdragon)
Young plants may be susceptible to slug or snail attack.

Asarum (Wild ginger)

Asplenium (Spleenwort)

Aster
Some Asters are more susceptible to slug damage than others – an *Aster lateriflorus* 'Prince' was demolished to a stalk within days of planting out. However, *Aster amellus*, *Aster* x *frikartii* and the Michaelmas Daisy *Aster novae-angliae* all come recommended as resistant both to slugs and the powdery mildew that attacks many asters. They make useful garden plants as their flowers in shades of white, pink or mauve appear late in the season.

Aster, China see *Callistephus*

Astilbe
The astilbes are summer-flowering perennials, available in shades of red, pink and white.

Astrantia (Masterwort)
Very popular border plants. The flowers are available in subtle shades of red, pink and white and can be dried.

Athyrium (Lady Fern)

Aubreta (often called *Aubretia*)
These ubiquitous little rockplants are often listed as slug resistant, but they can be attacked, and slugs seem to particularly enjoy the flower-buds.

Aucuba (Spotted Laurel)
Auricula
Garden auriculas may be attacked by slugs or snails.

Aurinia (Yellow Alyssum)
This golden-flowered rockplant like other members of the cabbage family, it may be set upon by caterpillars.

Autumn Crocus see *Colchicum*

Avens see *Geum*

B

Baby's Breath see *Gypsophila*
Balloon Flower see *Platycodon*

Ballota
These members of the mint family have aromatic, hairy leaves.

Bamboo
Banana Plant see *Musa*

Baptisia (Wild Indigo)
These herbaceous perennials prefer soil with a low lime content.

Barley see *Hordeum*

Basil see *Ocimum*

Bassia (*Kochia.* Summer Cypress, Burning Bush*)*
Generally used as foliage plants for bedding, these half-hardy annuals are green all summer and vibrant red in the autumn, they are great to extend the summer season.

Bay see *Laurus*

Beard Tongue see *Penstemon*

Bear's Breeches see *Acanthus*

Begonia
May be attacked by other pests and diseases.

Belladonna Lily see *Amaryllis*

Bellflower see *Campanula*

Bellwort see *Uvularia*

Bellis (Daisy)
These attractive little plants may be attacked by aphids.

Bergamot see *Monarda*

Berberis
Colourful and spiny shrubs.

Bergenia (Elephant's Ears)
Early-flowering and large-leaved.

Bidens

Billardiera
These climbers are not susceptible to slug or snail attack.

Bittersweet see *Celastrus*

Black-eyed Susan see *Thunbergia*

Blanket Flower see *Gaillardia*

Blazing Star see *Liatris*

Blechnum (Hard Fern)

Bleeding Heart see *Dicentra*

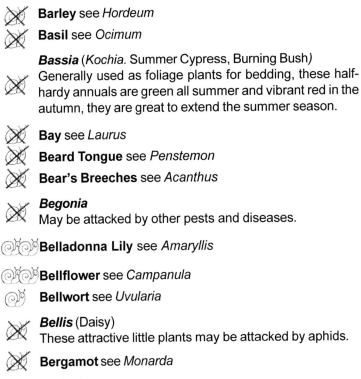

31

Bletilla (Garden Orchid)
These hardy orchids are not usually attacked by slugs or snails.

Blood Grass see *Imperata*

Bluebell see *Hyacinthoides*

Blue Spiraea see *Caryopteris*

Borago (Borage)
A pretty blue-flowered herb, borage has tough, prickly leaves and can seed itself quite freely.

Bottlebrush see *Callistemon*

Box see *Buxus*

Brachyglottis
Evergreen shrubs with yellow daisy-flowers.

Brachyscome (Swan River Daisy)
Usually grown in containers or hanging baskets.

Bridal Wreath see *Spiraea*

Briza (Quaking Grass)

Broom see *Cytisus*

Brugmansia (Angel's Trumpet)
When grown outdoors, angel's trumpets are susceptible to attack by a variety of pests, including slugs and snails.

Brunnera
Forgetmenot-like herbaceous perennials.

Buckler Fern see *Dryopteris*

Buddleja (Butterfly Bush)

Bugle see *Ajuga*

Bugloss see *Anchusa*

Burnet see *Sanguisorba*

Burning Bush see *Bassia*

Butterbur see *Petasites*

Butterfly Bush see *Buddleja*

Butterwort see *Pinguicula*

Buxus (Box)
Said to be effective against malaria, but contains toxic alkaloids. Little used medicinally today but often grown as edging plants.

Busy Lizzie see *Impatiens*

C

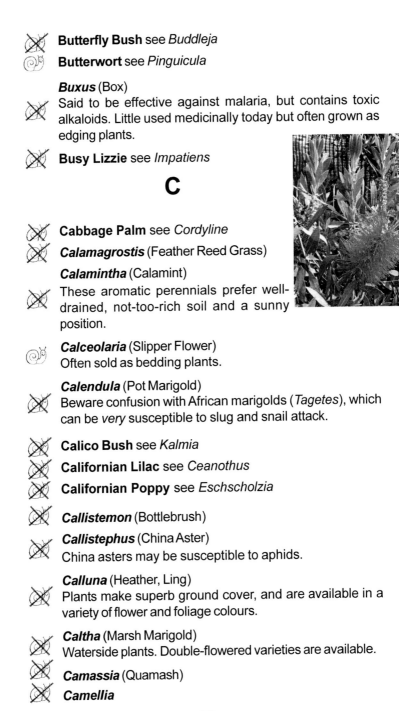

Cabbage Palm see *Cordyline*

Calamagrostis (Feather Reed Grass)

Calamintha (Calamint)
These aromatic perennials prefer well-drained, not-too-rich soil and a sunny position.

Calceolaria (Slipper Flower)
Often sold as bedding plants.

Calendula (Pot Marigold)
Beware confusion with African marigolds (*Tagetes*), which can be *very* susceptible to slug and snail attack.

Calico Bush see *Kalmia*

Californian Lilac see *Ceanothus*

Californian Poppy see *Eschscholzia*

Callistemon (Bottlebrush)

Callistephus (China Aster)
China asters may be susceptible to aphids.

Calluna (Heather, Ling)
Plants make superb ground cover, and are available in a variety of flower and foliage colours.

Caltha (Marsh Marigold)
Waterside plants. Double-flowered varieties are available.

Camassia (Quamash)

Camellia

Camomile *see Anthemis or Chamaemelum*

Aromatic, evergreen, camomile has an antiseptic anti-flammatory action and is soothing. Prefers light, sandy soil and a sunny position.

Campanula (Bellflower)

This is a large group of very attractive plants, and sadly, many of them are vulnerable to slug or snail attack. A *Campanula garganica* 'Dickson's Gold' was reduced to a stump in a matter of days. *Campanula zoysii* is said to be particularly susceptible. However, we can recommend the Serbian bellflower, *Campanula poscharskyana*, an evergreen, vigorous rockery plant. It flowers exuberantly and looks great trailing over a wall.

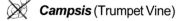

Campion see *Lychnis* and *Silene*

Campsis (Trumpet Vine)

Candytuft *see Iberis*

Canna (Indian Shot)

Cannas are exotic-looking plants, with a variety of interesting patterned and coloured leaves. They are generally too tender to live outdoors all year.

Cape Daisy see *Osteospermum*

Cape Fuchsia see *Phygelius*

Cape Gooseberry see *Physalis*

Cardamine

Cardiocrinum (Lily)

Cardoon see *Cynara*

Carex (Sedge)

Beware: some of them can be invasive.

Caryopteris (Blue Spiraea)

A lovely late-flowering shrub.

Catananche (Cupid's Dart)
Theattractive daisy-like flowers come in shades of purple-blue and white, and are suitable for drying for winter flower arrangements.

Catchfly see *Silene*

Catmint see *Nepeta*

Ceanothus (Californian Lilac)

Celastrus (Bittersweet)

Centaurea (Knapweed)
Among the knapweeds the perennial cornflower (*Centaurea montana)* and the pink-flowered *Centaurea dealbata* come specially recommended as slug and snail resistant. The perennial cornflower comes in a range of colours from purple-blue to pink to white.

Centranthus (Red Valerian)
These plants may suffer a certain amount of slug and snail nibbling in the spring, but they are so fast-growing, it doesn't seem to do any real harm. Beware: they can seed themselves quite freely.

Cephalaria

Cerastium
Snow in summer (*Cerastium tomentosum*) is a silver-leaved rockplant. Beware: it can be invasive.

Ceratostigma
Late-flowering shrubs.

Chaenomeles (Quince)

Chaerophyllum (Chervil)

Chamaemelum (Camomile)

***Chelone* (Turtlehead)**
Turtleheads are attractive late-flowering plants.

Chervil see *Anthriscus* or *Chaerophyllum*

Chilean Glory Vine see *Eccremocarpus*

China Aster see *Callistephus*

Chinese Lantern see *Physalis*

Chimonobambusa

Chionochloa (Tussock Grass)

Chionodoxa (Glory of the Snows)
Early-flowering and available in shades of violet-blue, pink and white, these bulbs are recommended as slug resistant.

Choisya (Mexican Orange Blossom)
An evergreen shrub which needs minimal pruning and can be grown as a hedge. Although prone to frost damage in exposed sites.

Christmas Box see *Sarcococca*

Chrysanthemum

Chusquea

Cimicifuga
Tall, back-of-border-plants that require a moist soil and some shade.

Cinquefoil see *Potentilla*

Cistus (Rockrose)
Cistus are attractive little shrubs, available in shades of pink and white. They are also drought resistant.

Clarkia (*Godetia*)
Recommended for summer bedding for its colourful display.

Clematis
Popular climbers.

Clintonia

Cobaea (Cup and Saucer Vine)
This climbing half-hardy annual may be attacked by aphids.

Codonopsis

Colchicum (Autumn Crocus)
If you want to know whether or not you've got a colchicum, or a true autumn-flowering crocus, count the stamens: crocuses have three and colchicums have six stamens.

Coleus see *Solenostemon*

Columbine see *Aquilegia*

Comfrey see *Symphytum*

Cone Flower see *Echinacea* or *Rudbeckia*

Consolida (Larkspur)
Annual delphiniums, otherwise known as larkspurs, are fast-growing plants with feathery leaves. Young plants may be vulnerable to attack. Sow the seed *in situ* in spring or autumn in mild gardens.

Convolvulus (Bindweed)
The grey-leaved silverbush (*Convolvulus cneorum*) is probably too hairy to interest slugs and snails.

Coral Bells see *Heuchera*

Cordyline (Cabbage Palm)
Popular, palm-like plants.

Coreopsis (Tickseed)

Coriandrum (Coriander)
Propagated from seed sown in spring. Used in cookery, the crushed seeds are also added to scented sachets and pot-pourri. Medicinal.

Corn Lily see *Ixia*

Cortaderia (Pampas Grass)
Love them or hate them, these grasses are undeniably striking. Pampas grasses are available with variegated leaves, and, for the smaller garden, you can buy dwarf forms.

Corydalis
The yellow-flowered *Corydalis lutea* is generally recommended as resistant – beware: it can seed itself everywhere, especially among paving.

Cosmos

Cotoneaster
Tiny green leaves in summer and red berries in autumn or winter. Likes ordinary well-drained soil. Tolerates dry, chalky or clay soil.

Cotton Lavender see *Santolina*

Cow Parsley see *Anthriscus*

Crambe

The spring shoots of these plants may be attacked by slugs or snails.

Cranesbill see *Geranium*

Creeping Jenny see *Lysimachia*

Creeping Snapdragon see *Asarina*

Crinum

These stunning bulbous plants require a warm, sheltered site.

Crocosmia (Montbretia)

There are many gorgeously-coloured varieties of *Crocosmia*, The tall, scarlet-flowered *Crocosmia* 'Lucifer' makes a particularly stunning border plant. Beware: the ordinary orange-flowered *Crocosmia* can be quite invasive.

Crocus

Birds often damage the flowers.

> In a hot spring or summer the dryness of the soil will reduce the amount of slug and snail damage.

Crocus, Autumn see *Colchicum*

Cup and Saucer Vine see *Cobaea*

Cupid's Dart see *Catananche*

Cup Flower see *Nierembergia*

Cyananthus

These plants are very susceptible to slug attack.

Cyclamen

There are species available that flower in all four seasons. They require partial shade.

Cynara (Cardoon)

Cyrtomium (Holly Fern)

Ferns are not attacked by slugs or snails.

Cytisus (Broom)

Minimal pruning necessary.

D

Daboecia

Daffodil see *Narcissus*

Dahlia
Dahlias are prone to slug attack, especially when newly planted.

Daisy see *Bellis*

Daisy Bush see *Olearia*

Daisy, Cape see *Osteospermum*

Daisy, Livingstone see *Dorotheanthus*

Daisy, Michaelmas see *Aster*

Daisy, Oxeye see *Leucanthemum*

Daisy, Shasta see *Leucanthemum*

Daisy, Swan River see *Brachyscome*

Dame's Violet see *Hesperis*

Daphne
These winter-flowering shrubs have glossy dark green foliage. It does well in deep, damp or dry shade and is not susceptible to slug or snail attack. All parts are toxic, and contact with the sap may irritate skin.

Darmera (Umbrella Plant)
A plant which makes a fine, spreading water plant. Fully hardy, grows in sun or shade and requires moist soil. Propagated by division in spring or by seed in autumn.

Davallia (Squirrel's Foot Fern)
Ferns are not attacked by slugs or snails.

Day Lily see *Hemerocallis*

Deadnettle see *Lamium*

Delphinium
These lovely, tall border plants, ideal for cutting, are sadly very susceptible to slug attack in spring. Delphiniums rarely need staking. Cutting and removal of dead flowerheads will induce further flowering.

Deschampsia (Hair Grass)
These grasses are not attacked by slugs or snails.

Deutzia
Unusually for shrubs, Deutzias may be attacked in spring.

Devil's Claw see *Physoplexis*

Dianthus (Pinks)
Some pinks are susceptible to slug damage, some are not. The Sweet William *(Dianthus barbatus)* may get damaged. In general, the grey-leaved pinks are not usually attacked.

Diascia

Dicentra (Bleeding Heart)
These attractive plants are fairly resistant to slug and snail attack.

Dicksonia (Tree Fern)
Slugs and snails do not attack these large, exotic ferns. Tree ferns require rather more special care than most of our recommended plants, but for sheer drama they are unbeatable.

Dierama (Angel's Fishing Rod)
These lovely plants come recommended as slug and snail resistant. They require full sun, but will not tolerate drought.

Digitalis (Foxglove)
One tall border plant that doesn't get bitten to pieces by slugs and snails, the foxglove, is available in a wide choice of colours, including primrose yellow and soft apricot. Beware: these plants are poisonous.

Dill see *Anethum*

Disporum (Fairy Bells)
Best suited to woodland gardens, these plants may be susceptible to slug attack. Fully hardy.

Many slug pellets are now rain and mould resistant so they keep on working in all weathers.

Dodecatheon (Shooting Star)
The spring shoots of these plants may be susceptible to attack.

Dog's Tooth Violet see *Erythronium*

Doronicum (Leopard's Bane)
Slugs and snails do not usually attack these perennials.

Dorotheanthus (Livingstone Daisy)
Slugs may attack seedlings and young plants.

Draba
These little rockplants may be attacked by slugs or snails.

Dracunculus (Dragon Arum)
Dragon arums are not attacked by slugs or snails. Beware: these tuberous perennials can be very invasive.

Dryopteris (Buckler Fern)
These ferns are not attacked by slugs or snails.

E

Echeveria
Echeverias are attractive, grey-leaved succulents that are not susceptible to slug or snail attack. They are drought resistant, but are not hardy enough to stay outdoors all year in some areas.

Echinacea (Cone Flower)
Slugs and snails attack these popular border plants, especially the spring shoots.

Echinops (Globe Thistle)
These excellent border plants are not attacked by slugs or snails. The plants are drought resistant.

Echium (Viper's Bugloss)
Fully hardy to frost tender. Slugs and snails do not usually attack these plants. Sow in spring or autumn.

Eccremocarpus (Chilean Glory Vine)
Easy to grow and especially lovely when rambling through other shrubs or climbing roses. Slugs and snails do not attack this attractive climber, which likes sun, shelter and light, well-drained soil. Tolerates dry or chalky soil.

Garden Plants that Slugs Won't Eat!

Edelweiss see *Leontopodium*

Edraianthus
Short-lived perennials. Fully hardy.

Elaeagnus
Attractive evergreen shrubs grown for their foliage and small, fragrant flowers.

Elephant's Ears see *Bergenia*

Elymus (*Elytrigia*)

Epimedium
The spring shoots of these plants may be attacked by slugs.

Eranthis (Winter Aconite)
These early-flowering perennials will grow in sun or partial shade.

Eremurus (Foxtail Lily)
Perennials requiring a sunny, sheltered site.

Erica (Heath)
These excellent ground cover plants are available in a variety of flower and leaf colours. Apart from the winter-flowering varieties, they require acid soil.

Erigeron (Fleabane)
All these come recommended as slug resistant, including the Mexican daisy, *Erigeron karvinskianus* – but beware, this one can be invasive, especially among paving slabs.

Erinus (Fairy Foxglove)
Rockplants need sun and well-drained soil. Self seeds freely.

Eriophyllum
Requires sun and well-drained soil. Propagate by division in spring or by seed in autumn. Frost Hardy.

Erodium (Storksbill)

Eryngium (Sea Holly)
The sea hollies make dramatic and colourful garden plants. They are drought resistant and the long-lasting flowerheads can be dried.

Erysimum (Wallflower)

Wallflowers' foliage can be attacked by a variety of pests, including slugs and snails. Seedlings and young plants are probably most susceptible, but generally they survive the onslaught and flower successfully.

Erythronium (Dog's Tooth Violet)

Escallonia

Colourful, evergreen shrubs, that make excellent hedging.

Eschscholzia (Californian Poppy)

These colourful annuals are generally drought resistant.

Eucomis (Pineapple Lily)

In severe winters protect with dead bracken.

Eulalia Grass see *Miscanthus*

Euonymus (Spindle)

Eupatorium

Requires full light or partial shade, but some species will prefer moist soil. Red spider mite and whitefly may be troublesome.

Euphorbia (Spurge)

Spurges have an irritant in their sap. They are excellent garden plants ranging from small ground-cover species to large, architectural border plants. *Euphorbia characias* and *Euphorbia griffithii* come specially recommended. Most of them are also drought resistant.

Euryops

These daisy-flowered evergreen shrubs are good for borders.

Evening Primrose see *Oenothera*

Everlasting Pea see *Lathyrus*

Exochorda

Does best in full sun and fertile, well-drained soil.

F

Fairy Bells see *Disporum*

Fairy Foxglove see *Erinus*

Fallopia
The mile-a-minute plant, *Fallopia baldschuanica,* is often sold as a useful plant to cover sheds or fences in a hurry. It does this, but beware: it may continue to grow to an enormous size.

Fan Flower see *Scaevola*

Fargesia
Plant this bamboo in dappled shade in fertile, moist soil for best results. They do not appreciate cold, drying winds.

Feather Grass see *Pennisetum* and *Stipa*

Feather Reed Grass see *Calamagrostis*

Felicia
These daisy-like, mainly blue flowers need full sun.

Fennel see *Foeniculum*

Ferns

Festuca (Fescue)
The popular blue fescue makes a striking foliage plant.

Feverfew see *Tanacetum*

Filipendula (Meadowsweet)
Filipendulas are available in shades of pink and white, and prefer damp soil.

Firethorn see *Pyracantha*

Flame Creeper see *Tropaeolum*

Flax see *Linum*

Fleabane see *Erigeron*

Flowering Currant see *Ribes*

Foam Flower see *Tiarella*

Foeniculum (Fennel)
The bronze fennel makes a striking border plant.

Forget-me-not see *Myosotis*

Forsythia
Spring flowering shrub. Fully hardy.

Fothergilla
These spring flowering shrubs need moist, peaty, acid soil.
Grows in semi-shade.

Foxglove see *Digitalis*

Foxglove, Fairy see *Erinus*

Foxtail Lily see *Eremurus*

Foxtail Millet see *Setaria*

Francoa
Frost hardy, these perennials need full
sun and well-drained soil.

French Marigold see *Tagetes*

Fritillaria (Fritillary)
Mainly bell-shaped flowers on leafy stems, these plants may
be attacked by slugs and snails.

Fuchsia
The hardy fuchsias make wonderful garden plants with a
long flowering season. They are available in a wide range of
flower shapes and colours, and also with variegated, golden
yellow or multi-coloured leaves. Beware: the leaves are
sometimes disfigured by fuchsia rust.

G

Gaillardia (Blanket Flower)
All gaillardias make good cut flowers, and are generally
drought resistant.

Galanthus (Snowdrop)

Galega (Goat's Rue)
Likes sun and well-drained soil. Staking required.

Galium (Woodruff)

This woodland plant is cultivated as ground cover and is fully hardy. Propagate by division in early spring or autumn.

Galtonia (Summer Hyacinth)

Striking, late-flowering, bulbous perennials. They may not be hardy enough to withstand the winter outdoors in cold areas.

Gardener's Garters see Phalaris

Garlic *see Allium*

Gaultheria

Gaura

A graceful pink or white-flowered perennial, Gaura lindheimen comes recommended as slug and snail resistant. It is a very useful late-flowering border plant.

Gazania (Treasure Flower)

These showy South African plants, often sold as summer bedding. The grey-leaved varieties such as 'Bicton Orange' and 'Aztec' are particularly tough.

Genista

Sometimes almost leafless, grown for their mass of small, pea-like flowers. It resents being transplanted.

Gentiana (Gentian)

Gerbera

Geranium (Cranesbill)

The hardy geraniums (not to be confused with *Pelargoniums),* often sold as bedding 'geraniums'. They vary from tiny sun-loving rockplants to substantial, shade-tolerant border plants - something to suit every garden.

Germander see *Teucrium*

Geum (Avens)

All the geums come recommended as slug resistant, and the scarlet-flowered *Geum chiloense* in particular.

Giant Rhubarb see *Gunnera*

Ginger Lily see *Hedychium*

Ginger, Wild see *Asarum*

Gladiolus
Slugs and snails do quite enjoy munching the leaves, though this is rarely enough to ruin the display.

Glaucidium

Globe Flower see *Trollius*

Globe Thistle see *Echinops*

Glory of the Snows see *Chionodoxa*

Glory Vine see *Eccremocarpus*

Glyceria (Reed Grass)
Beware: these plants can be invasive.

Goat's Beard see *Aruncus*

Goat's Rue see *Galega*

Godetia see *Clarkia*

Granny's Bonnets see *Aquilegia*

Grape Hyacinth see *Muscari*

Grasses

Griselinia

Gunnera
All the gunneras, including and especially the big water-loving giant rhubarbs require sun and moist soil.

Gypsophila (Baby's Breath)
The gypsophilas come with recommendations from some gardeners, and warnings from others. It may be that the spring shoots of perennial Gypsophila can be attacked, while the annuals are resistant.

H

Haberlea
Young plants may be susceptible to slug attack.

Hair Grass see *Deschampsia*

Hakonechloa (Hakone Grass)

Halimium

These attractive flowering shrubs are not susceptible to slug or snail attack.

Hard Fern see *Blechnum*

Hare's Tail Grass see *Lagurus*

Harlequin Flower see *Sparaxis*

Heath see *Erica*

Heather see *Calluna*

Hebe

Excellent evergreen shrubs.

Hedera (Ivy)

Snails seem particularly fond of lurking in ivy before attacking more susceptible plants.

Hedychium (Ginger Lily)

Helenium (Sneezeweed)

Helianthemum (Rockrose)

Helianthus (Sunflower)

Annual sunflowers are very susceptible to slug and snail attack as seedlings or as young plants. Slugs sometimes attack the flowers, too.

Helichrysum

The helichrysums have tough, hairy, often silvery leaves. The trailing varieties sold for use in containers or hanging baskets are excellent. Other helichrysums are grown for their everlasting flowers, which dry beautifully. They are all drought resistant.

Helictotrichon (Oat Grass)

Heliopsis

These late-flowering perennials do best in full sun. Requires full sun and any well-drained soil. Fully hardy.

Heliotropium (Cherry Pie)

Often grown as bedding, these plants need full sun.

Helleborus (Hellebore)

The Christmas rose, (*Helleborus niger*) seems to be more susceptible to slug attack than the popular later-flowering *Helleborus orientalis* hybrids, which are generally considered more resistant.

Hemerocallis (Day Lily)

These attractive plants may suffer a little damage to their new shoots, but in general they are fairly resistant.

Hen and Chickens Houseleek see *Jovibarba*

Hepatica

Slugs will eat both leaves and flowers.

Hesperis (Dame's Violet, Sweet Rocket)

These sweetly-scented perennials prefer a slightly shaded site and are available in shades of purple, pink and white. A wonderful cottage-garden plant.

Heuchera (Coral Bells)

Excellent foliage plants specialising in bronze and red tones.

X *Hibanobambusa*

Hibiscus

Colourful shrubs that are not damaged by slugs or snails.

Himalayacalamus

Holcus (Velvet Grass)

Holly Fern see *Cyrtonium*

Hollyhock see *Alcea*

Honesty see *Lunaria*

Honeysuckle see *Lonicera*

Hop see *Humulus*

Hordeum (Barley)

Hosta (Plantain Lily)

The decorative leaves of these plants are notoriously susceptible to slug damage. *Hosta* 'Invincible' may be less susceptible than most.

Houseleek see *Sempervivum*

Houstonia

Houttuynia
These ground-covering perennials require a moist soil.

Humulus (Hop)
The golden-leaved 'Aureus' is an impressive plant.

Hyacinthoides (Bluebell)

Hyacinthus (Hyacinth)
Unlike the bluebells, these are very susceptible to slug and snail attack.

Hydrangea

Hylomecon
Young plants may be susceptible to slug damage.

Hypericum (St. John's Wort)
The foliage is sometimes disfigured by rust fungus. The rose of sharon (*Hypericum calycinum*) can be invasive.

Hypsela
These plants are susceptible to slug and snail attack.

I

Iberis (Candytuft)
The perennial candytufts, such as the rockplant *Iberis sempervirens* are not usually attacked by slugs or snails, however the annual candytuft, *Iberis amara* is susceptible to slug damage.

Iceland Poppy see *Papaver*

Ice Plant see *Sedum*

Impatiens (Busy Lizzie)
The colourful busy lizzies sold as summer bedding are all slug and snail resistant. The New Guinea Hybrids come specially recommended.

Imperata (Blood Grass)

Incarvillea

Indigo, Wild see *Baptisia*

Indocalamus

Inula

Inula hookeri comes specially recommended. The plants are happy in sun or part shade.

Ionopsidium

Ipomoea (Morning Glory)
Support is needed. Thin out congested growth in spring. Whitefly and red spider mite may cause problems.

Iris

Young shoots of many irises may be attacked by slugs and snails, but in our experience this is not enough to ruin the display of flowers.

Ivy see *Hedera*

Ixia (Corn Lily)
Plant in autumn for spring and early summer flowers.

J

Jacob's Ladder see

Polemonium

Jasminum (Jasmine)

These lovely climbers, including the fabulously-scented *Jasminum officinale* and the winter jasmine (*Jasminum nudiflorum*) are not usually attacked by slugs or snails.

Jersey Lily see *Amaryllis*

Jerusalem Sage see *Phlomis*

Jovibarba (Hen and Chickens Houseleek)

Juncus (Rush)

K

Kalmia
These shrubs, including the popular calico bush (*Kalmia latifolia*) are not usually attacked by slugs or snails.

Kerria

Kirengeshoma

Knapweed see *Centaurea*

Knautia (Scabious)
These attractive perennials are also generally drought resistant.

Kniphofia (Red Hot Poker)
The flower stems of these very decorative plants may be attacked by slugs or snails.

L

Lady Fern see *Athyrium*

Lady's Mantle see *Alchemilla*

Lagurus (Hare's Tail Grass)

Lamb's Ears see *Stachys*

Lamium (Deadnettle)
Shade-loving plants that can become invasive.

Lantana

Larkspur see *Consolida*

Lathyrus (Peaflowers)
Seedlings and young plants of the sweet pea (*Lathyrus odoratus)* are an absolute magnet for slugs and snails, and the damage can be devastating to the garden. The everlasting peas (*Lathyrus latifolius* and *L. grandiflorus)* seem less susceptible, although their wild, trailing habit is not acceptable to all gardeners.

Laurel, Spotted see *Aucuba*

Laurentia

Laurus (Bay)
The fragrant leaves have many culinary uses. Grows in fertile, reasonably moist but well-drained soil.

Lavandula (Lavender)
The fragrant oils in lavender leaves are very useful plants which come in a variety of forms, sizes and colours, smell wonderful and are drought resistant.

Lavatera (Tree Mallow)

Lavender see *Lavandula*

Lemon Balm see *Melissa*

Leontopodium (Edelweiss)
These rockplants may be susceptible to slug attack.

Leopard's Bane see *Doronicum*

Leucanthemum

Leucojum (Snowflake)

Levisticum (Lovage)
Can be used fresh or dry for soups, stews, meat, fish or vegetable dishes.

Lewisia
Brightly-flowered rockplants. They require a well-drained site.

Leycesteria (Pheasant Berry)

Liatris (Blazing Star)
The young shoots of these plants may be nibbled in spring, they revive quite quickly and generally this does not prevent them flowering.

Libertia

Ligularia

Ligustrum (Privet)
Fully to frost hardy.

Lilac see *Syringa*

Lilac, Californian see *Ceanothus*

Lilium (Lily)
Slugs are just one of the pests and diseases these desirable plants suffer from. However, the lovely *Lilium regale* comes recommended as slug resistant.

Lily see also *Cardiocrinum*

Lily, Corn see *Ixia*

Lily, Day see *Hemerocallis*

Lily, Foxtail see *Eremurus*

Lily, Ginger see *Hedychium*

Lily, May see *Maianthemum*

Lily, Pineapple see *Eucomis*

Lily, Plantain see *Hosta*

Lily Turf see *Ophiopogon*

Lily, Wood see *Trillium*

Limnanthes* (Poached Egg Plant)
These cheerful annuals do best in full sun.

*****Limonium*** (Statice; Sea Lavender)
These plants make excellent cut or dried flowers.

*****Linaria*** (Toadflax)
Toadflaxes don't seem to attract slugs or snails at all. Specially recommended is the grey-green leaved purple toadflax, *Linaria purpurea*. Beware: this species can seed itself quite freely.

Ling see *Calluna*

Linum (Flax)
Linum are available in shades of red, pink and blue, and do best in full sun. The seeds are used as laxatives, in infusions for coughs.

*****Liriope***

*****Lithodora***

Livingstone Daisy see *Dorotheanthus*

*****Lobelia***
These popular plants are sadly susceptible to slug attack.

*****Lobularia*** (*Alyssum*; Sweet Alison)
Widely available, these little annuals are drought resistant.

*****Lonicera*** (Honeysuckle)

Loosestrife see *Lysimachia*

Loosestrife, Purple see *Lythrum*

 Lotus
Prefers sun and well-drained soil.

 Lovage see *Levisticum*

 Love-in-a-Mist see *Nigella*

Luma (Myrtle)
 A sweet smelling evergreen shrub, which has long been associated with weddings and included in bridal bouquets.

Lunaria (Honesty)
 An old-fashioned cottage garden plant. Varieties are available with white or purple flowers, and also with variegated leaves.

 Lungwort see *Pulmonaria*

Lupinus (Lupin)
 Lupins are sadly very susceptible to slug damage.

 Luzula (Woodrush)

Lychnis (Campion)
 The campions' young shoots are susceptible to slug attack in spring. However, the grey-leaved rose campion (*Lychnis coronaria*) seems to be more resistant.

Lysichiton (Skunk Cabbage)
 These waterside plants are not usually attacked by slugs or snails however snails are often found under their leaves.

Lysimachia (Loosestrife)
 The little trailing creeping jenny (*Lysimachia nummularia*) comes specially recommended. Beware: the yellow loosestrife (*Lysimachia punctata*) can be invasive.

Lythrum (Purple Loosestrife)
 Found to have antibacterial properties and recommended by modern herbalists for many ailments. Said to be soothing for skin irritations.

M

Macleaya (Plume Poppy)
A superb tall border plant.

Mahonia
Winter-flowering shrubs. Low growing varieties are excellent for ground cover.

Maianthemum (May Lily)

Maidenhair Fern see *Adiantum*

Maiden Pink see *Dianthus*

Malcolmia (Virginia Stock)
Easy-to-grow little annuals.

Malva (Mallow)
The musk mallow (*Malva moschata*), which is available with pink or white flowers comes specially recommended. It is generally drought resistant, too.

Marigold, Marsh see *Caltha*

Marigold, Pot see *Calendula*

Marjoram see *Origanum*

Marvel of Peru see *Mirabilis*

Masterwort see *Astrantia*

Matteucia (Ostrich Fern)

Matthiola (Stock)
These scented plants will not grow in acid soils. Beware: these plants are prone to aphids, flea beetle, clubroot, downy mildew and botrytis.

May Lily see *Maianthemum*

Meadow Rue see *Thalictrum*

Meadowsweet see *Filipendula*

Meconopsis
These perennials may be susceptible to a certain amount of spring damage from slugs, but in our experience the widely-available Welsh poppy (*Meconopsis cambrica*) never shows any sign of damage and self-seeds itself happily.

Melianthus

Melica (Melick)

Melissa (Lemon Balm)
The strong-smelling leaves keep this herb free of slugs and snails. Beware: it can self-seed itself very freely.

Milkwort see *Polygala*

Mentha (Mint)
Whilst very invasive a large deep pot of it can be placed into the ground to contain its growth. Useful in tisanes and medicinally as well as in cooking.

Mexican Orange Blossom see *Choisya*

Mexican Sunflower see *Tithonia*

Michaelmas Daisy see *Aster*

Mile-a-Minute Plant see *Fallopia*

Milium (Wood Millet)
The flat, golden-yellow leaves are attractive. Self seeds readily in shade.

Milk Thistle see *Silybum*

Mimulus (Monkey Flower, Musk)
These useful garden plants are often sold as bedding.

Mint see Mentha

Mirabilis (Marvel of Peru)
Likes full sun and a sheltered position.

Miscanthus (Eulalia Grass)
These attractive grasses make excellent border plants.

Mock Orange see *Philadelphus*

Molinia (Moor Grass)

Monarda (Bergamot)
The monardas are colourful herbaceous plants, many of them with scented leaves, and they come recommended as slug resistant. They are available in shades of purple, pink or white.

Monkey Flower see *Mimulus*

Monkshood see *Aconitum*

Montbretia see *Crocosmia*

Moor Grass see *Molinia*

Morina (Whorl Flower)

Morning Glory see *Ipomoea*

Mount Atlas Daisy see *Anacyclus*

Mouse Plant see *Arisarum*

Mullein see *Verbascum*

Musa (Banana Plant)
Outdoor varieties of these exotic plants are resistant to slug and snail attack.

Muscari (Grape Hyacinth)
Useful spring-flowering bulbs. They will tolerate some shade.

Musk see *Mimulus*

Musk Mallow see *Malva*

Myosotis (Forget-me-not)
These popular little spring-flowering plants are susceptible to mildew.

Myrrhis (Sweet Cicely)
This aniseed smelling herb grows under any conditions, in sun or shade, but prefers moist, humus-rich soil. An invasive plant which self-seeds and spreads rapidly.

Myrtle see *Luma*

N

Narcissus (Daffodil)
Daffodil leaves and bulbs are generally not eaten by slugs or snails. However they may attack the flowers themselves, sometimes demolishing them completely. Daffodils grown in containers seem generally less susceptible.

Nasturtium see *Tropaeolum*

Nemesia
Colourful annuals.

Nepeta (Catmint)
The scented leaves keep the slugs off these perennials, with *Nepeta* x *faassenii* coming specially recommended.

Nerine
These bulbous plants are useful in any garden at the end of summer.

New Zealand Flax see *Phormium*

Nicandra (Shoo Fly Plant)

Nicotiana (Tobacco Plant)

Nierembergia (Cup Flower)
Perennials that prefer sun and moist but well-drained soil.

Nigella (Love-in-a-Mist)
Pretty blue-flowered annuals, even as tiny seedlings. Beware: can seed themselves quite freely.

Nomocharis

O

Oat Grass see *Helictotrichon*

Obedient Plant see *Physostegia*

Ocimum (Basil)

Oenanthe (Water Dropwort)

Oenothera (Evening Primrose)
Excellent border plant that likes a dry, sunny spot, preferably on a light soil.

Olearia (Daisy Bush)
Evergreen shrub or tree, grown for their foliage and daisy-like flower heads. Provides good, very wind-resistant shelter.

Omphalodes
Very susceptible to slug and snail attack, especially *Omphalodes luciliae*.

Onoclea (Sensitive Fern)

Onopordum (Scotch Thistle)

Ophiopogon (Lily Turf)
Popular perennials. The grasslike foliage comes in a variety of colours and patterning, including almost black.

Orchid, Garden see *Bletilla*

Orchid, Poor Man's see *Schizanthus*

Oriental Poppy see *Papaver*

Origanum (Marjoram)
Tasty herbs with antiseptic medicinal properties.

Ornithogalum (Star of Bethlehem)

Osmanthus

Osmunda (Royal Fern)

Osteospermum (Cape Daisy)
These plants are widely available in a large choice of colours, with new ones appearing all the time, and are often presented as summer bedding, although they will overwinter in many parts of the country.

Ostrich Fern see *Mattheuccia*

Ourisia
Excellent for beds and walls. Needs shade and moist soil.

Oxalis

Oxeye Daisy see *Leucanthemum*

Ozothamnus

P

Pachysandra

Paeonia (Peony)
These glamorous plants are available in many shades of red, pink and white.

Pampas Grass see *Cortaderia*

Panicum

Pansy see *Viola*

Papaver (Poppy)

Poppy seedlings are sometimes attacked by slugs, but the oriental poppy *(Papaver orientale)* and the Iceland poppy *(Papaver nudicaule)* come recommended as resistant.

Paradisia

Requires a sunny site and fertile, well-drained soil.

Parahebe

Suitable for rock gardens. Frost hardy. Needs sun and well-drained soil.

Paris

Parsley see *Petroselinum*

Parthenocissus (Virginia Creeper)

Climbers not usually attacked by slugs or snails, although they may provide a good daytime hideout for snails.

Pasque Flower see *Pulsatilla*

Passiflora (Passionflower)

Pearly Everlasting see *Anaphalis*

Pelargonium (Geranium)

Pelargoniums purchased as summer bedding can be attacked, especially when first planted out. However, this is rarely sufficient to spoil the display. The scented-leaved pelargoniums, such as the lemon-scented 'Lady Plymouth', are much more resistant to slugs and snails.

Pennisetum (Feather Grass)

Penstemon (Beard Tongue)

Peony see *Paeonia*

Periwinkle see *Vinca*

Perovskia (Russian Sage)

These useful blue-flowered border perennials have the added benefit of being drought resistant.

Persicaria

Beware: they can become invasive.

Peruvian Lily see *Alstroemeria*

Petasites (Butterbur)

These perennials are not usually attacked by slugs or snails, including the much-planted winter heliotrope (*Petasites fragrans*). Beware: can be very invasive.

Petroselinum (Parsley)

Petunia

Phalaris (Reed Canary Grass)

Beware: these plants can be invasive. The variegated variety *picta* (gardeners' garters) can be a menace in a small garden.

Pheasant Berry see *Leycesteria*

Pheasant's Eye see *Adonis*

Phegopteris

Philadelphus (Mock Orange)
Sweet-scented shrubs.

Phillyrea

Phlomis (Jerusalem Sage)

Phlox
Phlox paniculata is generally considered to be resistant.

Phormium (New Zealand Flax)
Spectacular border plants.

Photinia

Phuopsis
These carpet-forming perennials come recommended as slug resistant.

Phygelius (Cape Fuchsia)
Slugs and snails do not usually attack these colourful plants.

Phyllodoce
These dwarf shrubs are not usually attacked by slugs or snails.

Phyllostachys

Physalis (Chinese Lantern; Cape Gooseberry)

Physoplexis
These plants may be susceptible to attack, especially the devil's claw (*Physoplexis comosa*).

Physostegia (Obedient Plant)

Phytolacca
Beware: they can be invasive.

Pieris

Pigroot see *Sisyrinchium*

Pimpernel see *Anagallis*

Pineapple Lily see *Eucomis*

Pinguicula (Butterwort)

Pinks see *Dianthus*

Pittosporum

Plantain Lily see *Hosta*

Platycodon (Balloon Flower)

Plectranthus
Slugs and snails do not usually attack these trailing container plants.

Pleioblastus
Beware: these plants can be invasive.

Pleione
These orchids can be grown outdoors in some parts of the country.

Plume Poppy see *Macleaya*

Poached Egg Plant see *Limnanthes*

Polemonium (Jacob's Ladder)
Useful border plants. The leaves are specially attractive and the flowers can be purple, mauve or white.

Polygala (Milkwort)

Polygonatum (Solomon's Seal)

These decorative, shade-loving plants are fully hardy to frost tender. Bears pendent clusters of bell-shaped, white flowers in late spring.

Polypodium (Polypody)

Grow in semi-shade and fibrous, moist but well-drained soil.

Polystichum (Shield Fern)

Poor Man's Orchid see *Schizanthus*

Poppy see *Papaver*

Poppy, Welsh see *Meconopsis*

Portulaca (Sun Plant)

These half-hardy annuals are popular bedding plants.

Potato Vine see *Solanum*

Pot Marigold see *Calendula*

Potentilla (Cinquefoil)

The vibrant, vermilion red flowers of 'Marian Red Robin', flowers from May to October. It does best in partial shade.

Prairie Mallow see *Sidalcea*

Pratia

Some species may be invasive but generally grown for their mass of star-shaped flowers.

Primula

The primulas get a mixed review. We have never had any problems with our primroses (*Primula vulgaris*), but the popular polyanthus hybrids are sometimes attacked. See also *Auricula*.

Privet see *Ligustrum*

Prostanthera

Prunella (Self-heal)

A herb with an ancient history in Chinese herbalism.

Pseudosasa

Pterocephalus

Pulmonaria (Lungwort)
Often called Lungwort are very useful spring-flowering shade-tolerant plants. A useful substitute for hostas in a slug-infested garden. Their leaves and stems are covered in bristly hairs that make them unpalatable to slugs and snails.

Pulsatilla (Pasque Flower)
Pasque flowers are early-flowering rockery plants.

Purple Bell Vine see *Rhodochiton*

Puschkinia

Pyracantha (Firethorn)

Q

Quaking Grass see *Briza*
Quamash see *Camassia*
Quince see *Chaenomeles*

R

Ramonda
Ranunculus
Raoulia
These perennials require a warm, sunny site.

Red Hook Sedge see *Uncinia*
Red Hot Poker see *Kniphofia*
Red Valerian see *Centranthus*
Reed Canary Grass see *Phalaris*
Reed Grass *see Glyceria*
Rhodiola (*Roseroot*)
Rhodochiton (Purple Bell Vine)
Rhododendron
Unlike most shrubs, some rhododendrons may have their new growth attacked in spring.

Garden Plants that Slugs Won't Eat!

Rhodohypoxis

Ribes (Flowering Currant)

Rockcress see *Arabis*

Rock Jasmine see *Androsace*

Rockrose see *Cistus* and *Helianthemum*

Rodgersia

Romneya (Tree Poppy)
Slug and snails do not usually attack these perennials.

Rosa (Rose)

Roscoea
The spring shoots of these plants may be attacked.

Rose Campion see *Lychnis*

Roseroot see *Rhodiola*

Rosmarinus (Rosemary).
Although snails may shelter in the branches of rosemary plants on hot days, neither they nor slugs show any interest in eating the leaves or flowers. These superb, drought-resistant garden plants are available with blue, mauve, pink or white flowers, and in upright and trailing forms. Highly recommended.

Royal Fern see *Osmunda*

Rudbeckia (Coneflower)
Late summer flowering plants. *Rudbeckia fulgida* and its cultivars, with flowers of a startling golden yellow come specially recommended.

Rue see *Ruta*

Rush see *Juncus*

Russian Sage see *Perovskia*

Ruta (Rue)
Irritants in the sap keep slugs and snails off this drought-resistant perennial. Beware: some people are susceptible to the irritants, too. Aromatic, with insect-repellent properties. Leaves may be dried for adding to pot-pourri.

S

 St. John's Wort see *Hypericum*

Salvia (Sage)

 The handsome *Salvia* x *suberba* comes specially recommended. The annual salvias sold as bedding seem to be much less resistant.

 Sanguisorba (Burnet)

Santolina (Cotton Lavender)

 Useful and drought-resistant dwarf shrub with silver-grey foliage.

Saponaria (Soapwort)

 The little rockplant Tumbling Ted (*Saponaria ocymoides*) has hairy foliage that is rarely damaged.

 Sarcococca (Christmas Box)
Sweetly-scented shrubs.

 Sasa

 Sasaella
Beware: these plants can be invasive.

 Satureya (Savory)

Saxifraga (Saxifrage)

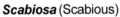 Silver saxifrage (*Saxifraga cochlearis*) is very attractive to slugs which feed on the foliage, but *Saxifraga* x *urbium* (London pride) and the similar *Saxifraga umbrosa* both come recommended as slug resistant.

Scabiosa (Scabious)

 Some scabious may suffer a certain amount of slug damage, but *Scabiosa caucasica* comes recommended as specially resistant.

 Scabious see *Knautia* or *Scabiosa*

 Scaevola (Fan Flower)

Schizanthus (Poor Man's Orchid)

 Grown for their showy flowers they need a sunny, sheltered position in well-drained, fertile, soil.

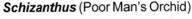

Schizophragma
Climbers (tie young plants to supports).

Schizostylis
Requires sun and moist soil.

***Scilla* (Squill)**
Pretty early flowering bulbs.

Scotch Thistle see *Onopordum*

Sea Holly see *Eryngium*

Sea Lavender see *Limonium*

Sedge see *Carex*

Sedum (Stonecrop)
The small rockery sedums are rarely attacked, including the yellow-flowered *Sedum kamtschaticum*, the red-flowered *Sedum spurium* and the grey-leaved *Sedum spathulifolium* 'Cape Blanco'.

Semiarundinaria

Sempervivum (Houseleek)
Houseleeks are evergreen, easy to grow, and there are many varieties to choose from. Lovely in troughs or containers.

Senecio
Shrub varieties are excellent for coastal gardens. Fully hardy to frost tender.

Self-heal see *Prunella*

Sensitive Fern see *Onoclea*

Sesleria

Setaria (Foxtail Millet)
Moderately fast-growing grasses.

Shasta Daisy see *Leucanthemum*

Shield Fern see *Polystichum*

Shibataea

Shoo Fly Plant see *Nicandra*

Shooting Star see *Dodecatheon*

Shortia
Difficult to grow in hot, dry climates. Needs shade or semi-shade.

 Sidalcea (Prairie Mallow)
This strikingly lovely, tall border plant is available in flower colours from rose pink to white.

 Silene (Campions and Catchflies)

 Silverbush see *Convolvulus*

 Silybum (Milk Thistle)

Sisyrinchium (Pigroot)
 There are several species and varieties of pigroot commonly available. *Sisyrinchium* 'Aunt May' is a good border plant with lovely variegated iris-like leaves. For the rockery or container garden there is the purple flowered *Sisyrinchium* 'E K Balls' and the slightly larger yellow-flowered *Sisyrinchium brachypus.*

Skimmia
 Too much sun or poor soil may cause chlorosis in these popular aromatic shrubs.

 Skunk Cabbage see *Lysichiton*

Slipper Flower see *Calceolaria*

Smilacina

Snapdragon see *Antirrhinum*

Snapdragon, Creeping see *Asarina*

Sneezeweed see *Helenium*

Snowberry see *Symphoricarpos*

Snowdrop see *Galanthus*

Snowflake see *Leucojum*

Snow in Summer see *Cerastium*

Soapwort see *Saponaria*

Solanum
This large group of plants, including the potato vine (*Solanum crispum*) are all resistant to slugs and snails.

Soldanella

Solenostemon (Coleus)

Usually grown as annuals, these striking perennials come in a variety of foliage colours and patterning.

Solidago (Golden rod)

Golden rods are mostly medium to tall border plants with a cottage-garden look. If you like the look, but need something smaller, there are dwarf varieties available.

Solomon's Seal see *Polygonatum*

Spanish Broom see *Spartium*

Sparaxis (Harlequin Flower)

Spartium (Spanish Broom)

Needs trimming in early spring to maintain a compact habit.

Speedwell see *Veronica*

Spiderwort see *Tradescantia*

Spindle see *Euonymus*

Spiraea (Bridal Wreath)

Grown for their mass of small flowers and, in some species, their foliage.

Spiraea, Blue see *Caryopteris*

Spleenwort see *Asplenium*

Spotted Laurel see *Aucuba*

Spurge see *Euphorbia*

Squill see *Scilla*

Squirrel's Foot Fern see *Davallia*

Stachys

The thick, woolly leaves of lamb's ears (*Stachys byzantina*) make it unattractive to slugs and snails.

Star of Bethlehem
see *Ornithogalum*

Statice see *Limonium*

Stephanandra

Sternbergia

Stipa (Feather Grass)

These grasses, include the popular golden oat (*Stipa gigantea*).

Stock see *Matthiola*

Stock, Virginia see *Malcolmia*

Stokesia (Stokes' Aster)

Stonecrop see *Sedum*

Storksbill see *Erodium*

Strobilanthes

These perennials prefer semi-shade.

Summer Cypress see *Bassia*

Summer Hyacinth see *Galtonia*

Sunflower see *Helianthus*

Sunflower, Mexican see *Tithonia*

Sun Plant see *Portulaca*

Swan River Daisy

see *Brachyscome*

Sweet Cicely see *Myrrhis*

Sweet Pea see *Lathyrus*

Sweet Rocket see *Hesperis*

Sweet William see *Dianthus*

Symphyandra

Short-lived, summer-flowering perennials which may suit large rock gardens and the bases of banks.

Symphoricarpos (Snowberry)

Grown for their clusters of showy, long-persistent fruits.

Symphytum (Comfrey)

The leaves are high in potash and make a good garden fertilizer and compost activator.

Syringa (Lilac)

Extremely fragrant shrubs. Needs sun.

T

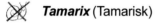**Tagetes** (French and African Marigolds)
These little plants, sold as summer bedding, often end up as a single stalk surrounded by slug pellets. They stand a better chance of survival if grown in tubs.

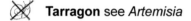**Tamarix** (Tamarisk)

Tanacetum (Feverfew, Tansy)
Many of the tanacetums have scented leaves, and some are silver-grey and hairy for good measure. The golden feverfew (*Tanacetum parthenium* 'Aureum') is an excellent garden plant.

Tarragon see *Artemisia*

Telekia
Herbaceous perennials.

Tellima
Shade-tolerant perennials.

Teucrium (Germander)
The germanders have hairy, often aromatic leaves.

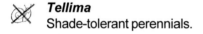

Thalictrum (Meadow Rue)
Tall border plant *Thalictrum aquilegifolium* comes specially recommended.

Thamnocalamus

Thistle, Globe see *Echinops*

Thrift see *Armeria*

Thunbergia (Black-eyed Susan)
Slugs and snails do not usually trouble these lovely climbing plants.

Thymus (Thyme)
Small scented herb.

Tiarella (Foam Flower)
Evergreen perennials. They prefer to grow in partial shade.

Tickseed see *Coreopsis*

Tigridia (Tiger Flower)
Spectacular, late-flowering bulbous plants.

 Tithonia (Mexican Sunflower)
 Toadflax see *Linaria*

 Toad Lily see *Tricyrtis*
 Tobacco Plant see *Nicotiana*

 Trachelospermum
Evergreen, sweet-scented, twining climbers. Frost hardy.

 Tradescantia (Spiderwort)
Some spiderworts are susceptible to slugs in spring, but
Tradescantia virginiana comes recommended as resistant.

 Treasure Flower see *Gazania*

 Tree Fern see *Dicksonia*

 Tree Mallow see *Lavatera*

 Tree Poppy see *Romneya*

 Tricyrtis (Toad Lily)

Trillium (Wood Lily)
 Medicinal perennial used as an
antiseptic, astringent herb, the plant
requires moist soil and partial shade.

Triteleia
These attractive plants, grown from
 corms, need semi-shade and moist, peaty, neutral to acid
soil. Fully hardy.

Tritonia
 These bulbous plants will only grow well in mild areas. Dry
off once the leaves start dying back in summer, (winter for
T. rubrolucens).

 Trollius (Globe Flower)
These bulbous plants require a moist soil.

Tropaeolum
 These lovely plants, including the nasturtium (*Tropaeolum
majus*) and the flame creeper (*T.* speciosum) are all slug
and snail resistant.

Garden Plants that Slugs Won't Eat!

Trumpet Vine see *Campsis*

Tulipa (Tulip)
Requires a sunny position.

Turtlehead see *Chelone*

Tussock Grass see *Chionochloa*

U

Umbrella Plant see *Darmera*

Uncinia (Red Hook Sedge)
An attractive red-leaved perennial, this sedge is perfect for the modern garden, it also does well in containers.

Uvularia (Bellwort)
These perennials thrive best in moist woodlands.

V

Valerian, Red see *Centranthus*

Valeriana (Valerian)
These perennials grow best in damp, fertile soil in a sunny position. Medicinal sedative properties and aromatic.

Vancouveria

Velvet Grass see *Holcus*

Veratrum
Ideal for woodland gardens.

Verbascum (Mullein)
These plants are generally drought tolerant. Beware: can be attacked by caterpillars of the mullein moth.

Verbena
These plants, including the popular tall, purple-flowered vervain (*Verbena bonariensis*) all come recommended as slug and snail resistant.

Veronica (Speedwell)
The lovely spiked speedwell (*Veronica spicata*) comes specially recommended and is available with flowers in purple-blue, pink or white.

Vervain see *Verbena*

Viburnum

Vinca (Periwinkle)
These little evergreen, trailing sub-shrubs may become invasive.

Viola (Violet, Pansy)

Virginia Creeper see *Parthenocissus*

Virginia Stock see *Malcolmia*

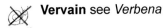

W

Wahlenbergia

Wallflower see *Erysimum*

Water Dropwort see *Oenanthe*

Weigela
Preferring sunny, fertile soil these shrubs are not usually attacked by slugs or snails. To maintain shape and strength, prune out a few older branches to ground level, after flowering each year.

Welsh Poppy see *Meconopsis*

Whorl Flower see *Morina*

Wild Ginger see *Asarum*

Wild Indigo see *Baptisia*

Winter Aconite see *Eranthis*

Winter Heliotrope see *Petasites*

Wisteria
Glorious twining climbers suitable for walls and pergolas. Likes full sun. Prune after flowering and again in late winter.

Wood Lily see *Trillium*

Wood Millet see *Milium*

Woodruff see *Galium*

Garden Plants that Slugs Won't Eat!

Woodrush see *Luzula*

Woodwardia
Ferns are not attacked by slugs or snails.

Wormwood see *Artemisia*

Y

Yarrow see *Achillea*

Yellow Alyssum see *Aurinia*

Yucca

Yushania

Z

Zantedeschia (Arum)
Usually evergreen, these popular perennials prefer a moist soil and full sun.

Zauschneria
Perennials usually grown for their mass of flowers.

Zinnia
The large, dahlia-like flowerheads are excellent for cutting. Like full sun. Dead-head regularly.

Advice on Fruit and Vegetables

Nearly all kinds of fruit and vegetables are attacked by pests, some of them very specialised. It's obvious, when you think about it, that the plants we use for food will also be enjoyed by other animals. Fruit that grows on trees is not usually slug susceptible, but otherwise it's difficult to give hard and fast recommendations. We can offer guidance on a few of the more slug-resistant herbaceous vegetables - but bear in mind that even these might be vulnerable to other pests.

Apple - mostly resistant to snails and slugs the apple may produce many other problems, i.e Scab, sawfly and several viruses.

Asparagus - never let the asparagus bed dry out and don't harvest the shoots for the first three years, but cut off the yellow foliage in the autumn. Slugs  and earwigs and the well-known asparagus beetle can be a yearly problem.

Beetroot - beetroot is a crop relatively free of pests and diseases, including slugs. However, Beet leaf, commonly known as Swiss chard, is a popular habitat for slugs.

Beans (Broad, French and Runner beans) - whilst all need a sunny aspect and a rich, well-manured soil, the leaves can be free of slug attack if planting is started in a greenhouse We spray a garlic wash over beans when first planting them out to help deter slugs & snails.

.

Garden Plants that Slugs Won't Eat!

Blackcurrants - not susceptible to slugs and snails

Brassicas (cabbages) - winter brassicas - kale, sprouts, cauliflower and spring cabbage are rather less prone to slug damage, but many varieties can get clubroot mildly.

Carrot - free from slug and snail attack but prone to the carrot fly which lays its eggs on the carrot. The larvae then burrow into the roots, devastating the crop.

Celery - strong-smelling enough to deter slug attacks.

Courgette - prone to slug attack.

Garlic/onions - these vegetables are strong-smelling enough to deter any slug attacks. It is now widely recognised that a garlic wash will deter many slugs from munching on new plants.

Jerusalem Artichokes - slugs rarely attack them, although Globe Artichokes can suffer from Botrytis.

Marrows - a favourite of slugs, particularly those laying on the ground.

Peaches - may develop Peach leaf curl which is a Fungus. Once ripened they may be susceptible to slugs, especially in windfalls.

Peas - slugs like peas, as do many other bugs such as pea moth and the pea thrip. In very damp weather pea leaves and pods may go white with mildew and then rot.

Pear - pears are more inclined to suffer from canker and the codling moth than from any problems with slugs and snails.

Potatoes - the more slug resistant potato varieties include: Charlotte, Estima, Kestrel, Pentland Dell, Pentland Falcon, Pentland Ivory, Pentland Squire, Slemster, Stourmont Enterprise and Wilja. For best results, plant a resistant variety, and harvest the minute they're ready. Leaving them in the ground too long is providing irresistible temptations to slugs and eelworm.

Raspberries - rarely attacked by either slugs or snails.

Salad Leaves - sadly, baby leaf salads are as attractive to slugs and snails as they are to us. Lettuces are very susceptible to slug attack, though red lettuce and continuity lettuce are said to be a little less vulnerable than some. Endive and cornsalad seem even less susceptible, and landcress and rocket come recommended as resistant.

Spinach - susceptible to slug attack in young leaves.

Strawberry - slugs are partial to the odd strawberry although the plants are more likely to be attacked by the Strawberry beetle. Plenty of straw around the base of each plant helps to keep slugs at bay.

> Slugs go scrumping and attack in the dark of night when ripe red strawberries are in season, particularly in June and July.

Swiss Chard - hardy enough to be resistant to most pests and diseases.

Tomatoes rarely seem to suffer slug damage.

> You will need to protect your French beans from slugs and snails with beer traps or organic pellets.

Using Slug Resistant Plants in your Garden

This section draws on the author's selection of the best slug and snail resistant plants you can choose for your garden. Plants have been chosen for their useful features, including shade tolerance, ability to grow in damp places, groundcovering qualities, and early and late flowering times.

There are also lists for summer bedding, rockplants and border plants gauged according to size, as well as selections for single-colour gardens, foliage plants and dried flowers. Quite a few of the plants are multi-talented and appear in more than one of the recommendation lists.

The suggested selections are all freely available, and can be found in most garden centres. Most of the recommendations are plants that will grow in a reasonably sunny situation in most types of soil, with one or two clearly-labelled exceptions. This does not, of course, apply to the lists for shady or damp conditions.

Common names have been included, where plants have them.

For further details about individual plants, see the Directory of Plants, (*See page 25*).

Groundcover

Groundcover plants, that is, lowish-growing plants that spread and cover an area of garden, are almost by definition invasive. They may continue to spread happily long after they have covered the area you want filled, so some of these come with an invasion warning attached. In particular, snow-in-summer (*Cerastium tomentosum*), cypress spurge (*Euphorbia cyparissias*) and dead-nettles (*Lamium*) can outstay their welcome and be tricky to eradicate. That said, they will do a splendid job covering a bare patch, or helping to fill in a new garden in a hurry.

• *Ajuga* (Bugle) will tolerate shade
• *Alchemilla* (Lady's Mantle)
• *Calluna* (Ling, Heather) needs lime-free soil

- *Cerastium tomentosum* (Snow-in-Summer)
- *Erica* (Heath) needs lime-free soil, except winter-flowering varieties
- *Euphorbia cyparissias* (Cypress Spurge)
- *Houttuynia* likes moist soil
- *Lamium* (Deadnettle) will tolerate shade
- *Ophiopogon* (Lily Turf)
- *Pachysandra* likes shade
- *Saponaria ocymoides* (Tumbling Ted)
- *Sedum kamtschaticum* (Yellow Stonecrop)
- *Thymus* (Thyme)

Annuals and Summer Bedding

Many of the plants that come to grief through slug and snail attacks are annuals or plants bought as summer bedding. It is particularly galling, when you have spent time and money choosing gloriously perfect plants in the garden centre, and lovingly planted them out, to find them reduced overnight to a collection of mangled stumps. And it's downright heartbreaking when you've raised them from seed yourself. Our selections will help to put an end to this annual disappointment, whether you grow from seed, or buy ready-grown from the garden centre.

- Snapdragon (*Antirrhinum*)
- *Bassia* (*Kochia*; Burning Bush)
- *Begonia*
- *Bellis* (Daisy)
- *Calendula* (Pot Marigold)
- *Clarkia* (*Godetia*)
- *Eschscholzia* (Californian Poppy)
- *Gazania* (Treasure Flower)
- *Helichrysum*
- *Heliotropium* (Cherry Pie)
- *Limnanthes* (Poached Egg Plant)
- *Limonium sinuatum* (Sea Lavender; Statice)
- *Lobularia* (*Alyssum*; Sweet Alison)
- *Malcolmia* (Virginia Stock)
- *Matthiola* (Stock)
- *Myosotis* (Forgetmenot)
- *Nigella* (Love-in-a-Mist)

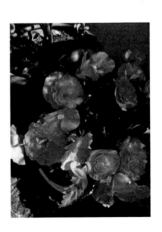

• *Osteospermum* (Cape Daisy)
• *Papaver nudicaule* (Iceland Poppy)

Plants for Shady Conditions

Coping with shade is one of the commonest garden problem areas. Most often this does not involve the kind of deep and permanent shade found in woodlands, but a combination of sun and shade, varying according to time of day. With this in mind, this selection includes many plants that will tolerate a degree of sunshine. Among the ivies, it's worth noting that the variegated cultivars may lose some of their attractive colouring if they are kept in deep shade. Specially recommended come the hardy geraniums, with most of the larger species and varieties being shade tolerant. We have listed two ferns by name, but there are many others that will happily grow in shady conditions.

• *Aconitum* (Monkshood) likes moist soil
• *Ajuga* (Bugle)
• *Alchemilla* (Lady's Mantle)
• *Anemone* x *hybrida* (Japanese Anemone)
• *Astrantia* (Masterwort)
• *Chionodoxa* (Glory of the Snows)
• *Digitalis* (Foxglove)
• *Euphorbia griffithii* (Spurge)
• *Geranium* (Cranesbill)
• *Hedera* (Ivy)
• *Heuchera* (Coral Bells)
• *Lamium* (Deadnettle)
• *Matteuccia* (Ostrich Fern) likes damp ground
• *Osmunda* (Royal Fern) likes damp ground
• *Pulmonaria* (Lungwort)
• *Saxifraga* x *urbium* (London Pride)
• *Tellima*
• *Vinca* (Periwinkle)

Copperstrips and various glues around pots help to keep slugs and snails off the plants but it is not an effective method of control.

Damp Soil Conditions:

Plants that grow in ponds and streams generally don't have too many problems with slugs and snails because they are inaccessible. This list covers plants that grow in moist conditions or on the margins of pools and streams. Some, like the marsh marigold will also grow in the water itself. The gunneras come with the warning that they can become very large plants, and so may not be suitable for the smaller garden.

- *Aruncus* (Goat's Beard)
- *Astilbe*
- *Caltha* (Marsh Marigold)
- *Dierama* (Angel's Fishing Rods)
- *Euphorbia griffithii* (Spurge)
- *Filipendula* (Meadowsweet)
- *Gunnera* (Giant Rhubarb)
- *Houttuynia* likes moist soil
- *Lysimachia* (Loosestrife)
- *Lythrum salicaria* (Purple Loosestrife)
- *Matteuccia* (Ostrich Fern)
- *Osmunda* (Royal Fern)
- *Zantesdeschia* (Arum)

Rockeries and Containers

Our selections here are generally tough little plants that will not need constant attention. With the exception of creeping jenny (*Lysimachia nummularia*) and the two sisyrhinchiums, they are all pretty drought-resistant, too, which is a useful feature for a container plant. Snow-in-summer (*Cerastium tomentosum*) comes with its usual warning: can be invasive.

- *Armeria* (Thrift)
- *Aurinia* (Golden Alyssum)
- *Campanula poscharskyana* (Serbian Bellflower)
- *Cerastium tomentosum* (Snow-in-Summer)
- *Crocus*
- *Dianthus*, alpine hybrids only

Garden Plants that Slugs Won't Eat!

- *Echeveria*
- *Erica* (Heath) requires acid soil
- *Erigeron karvinskianus* (Mexican Daisy)
- *Euphorbia myrsinites* (Spurge)
- *Geranium* (Cranesbill)
- *Helianthemum* (Rockrose)
- *Helichrysum*
- *Iberis sempervirens* (Perennial Candytuft)
- *Jovibarba* (Hen and Chickens Houseleek)
- *Lobularia* (*Alyssum*; Sweet Alison)
- *Lysimachia nummularia* (Creeping Jenny)
- *Muscari* (Grape Hyacinth)
- *Saponaria ocymoides* (Tumbling Ted)
- *Sedum spurium* (Red Stonecrop)
- *Sedum spathulifolium* (Stonecrop)
- *Sempervivum* (Houseleek)
- *Sisyrinchium 'E K Balls'*
- *Sisyrinchium brachypus*

Borders plants small, medium and large

The word 'borders' covers a broad range of situations, from a narrow edging strip to a full-blown herbaceous border three or four metres wide, so we have divided our border plant recommendations according to size.

Small: Under 15 cm tall

These plants have all proved useful as 'front-of-border' or edging plants. They are all under 15 cm tall, or have low-growing varieties available. Many of these will self-seed. If you find this a problem, then bugle (*Ajuga*), rockrose (*Helianthemum*), candytuft (*Iberis sempervirens*) and grape hyacinth (*Muscari)* are your best choices.

- *Ajuga* (Bugle)
- *Alchemilla* (Lady's Mantle)
- *Allium moly* (Golden Garlic)
- *Armeria* (Thrift)
- *Aurinia* (Golden Alyssum)

- *Dianthus deltoides* (Maiden Pink)
- *Erigeron karvinskianus* (Mexican Daisy)
- *Geranium* (Cranesbill)
- *Helianthemum* (Rock rose)
- *Iberis sempervirens* (Perennial Candytuft)
- *Lobularia* (*Alyssum*; Sweet Alison)
- *Muscari* (Grape Hyacinth)
- *Myosotis* (Forgetmenot)

Medium: 15cm to 1m tall
Individual varieties may be a little taller.

- *Allium christophii*
- *Anaphalis* (Pearly Everlasting)
- *Anemone hupehensis* (Japanese Anemone)
- *Artemisia* (Wormwood)
- *Aster amellus*
- *Astrantia*
- *Calluna* (lime-free soil)
- *Catananche*
- *Centaurea dealbata* (Knapweed)
- *Centaurea montana* (Perennial Cornflower)
- *Crocosmia* (Montbretia)
- *Digitalis* (Foxglove)
- *Erica* (Heaths) require lime-free soil, except winter-flowering varieties
- *Eryngium* (Sea Holly)
- *Euphorbia amygdaloides* 'Purpurea' (Wood Spurge)
- *Gaillardia* (Blanket Flower)
- *Geranium* (Cranesbill)
- *Geum chiloense* (Avens)
- *Helianthemum* (Rockrose)
- *Heuchera* (Coral Bells)
- *Linaria purpurea* (Purple Toadflax)
- *Lunaria annua* (Honesty)
- *Miscanthus* (Eulalia Grass)
- *Monarda* (Bergamot; Bee Balm)
- *Nepeta* x *faasenii* (Catmint)
- *Paeonia* (Peony)

A slug has a life span of several years, and every year it will grow bigger.

Garden Plants that Slugs Won't Eat!

- *Papaver orientale* (Oriental Poppy)
- *Phlomis fruticosa* (Jerusalem Sage)
- *Polemonium foliosissimum* (Jacob's Ladder)
- *Rudbeckia fulgida* (Coneflower)
- *Salvia x superba* (Sage)
- *Sedum* 'Autumn Joy' (properly called 'Herbstfreude')
- *Sidalcea* (Prairie Mallow)
- *Veronica spicata* (Spiked Speedwell)

Tall: 1m or taller

Beware: some of these can grow very big indeed, notably the pampas grasses (*Cortaderia*). There are smaller, less expansive varieties available, so check the ultimate height and spread carefully before you buy.

- *Acanthus* (Bear's Breeches)
- *Achillea filipendulina* (Golden Yarrow)
- *Aconitum* (Monkshood)
- *Anemone* x *hybrida* (Japanese Anemone)
- *Aster* x *frikartii*
- *Aster* x *novae-angliae* (Michaelmas Daisy)
- *Cortaderia* (Pampas Grass)
- *Crocosmia* 'Lucifer'
- *Dierama* (Angel's Fishing Rods)
- *Digitalis*
- *Eryngium* (Sea Holly)
- *Euphorbia characias* (Spurge)
- *Foeniculum vulgare* 'Purpureum (Bronze Fennel)
- *Fuchsia magellanica* 'Versicolor'
- *Gaura*
- *Malva moschata* (Musk Mallow)
- *Perovskia* (Russian Sage)
- *Phygelius* (Cape Fuchsia)
- *Solidago canadensis* (Golden Rod)
- *Stipa gigantea* (Golden Oat)
- *Thalictrum aquilegifolium* (Meadow Rue)
- *Verbena bonariensis* (Vervain)

Scented Plants

This selection will also include all the herbs (see page 98).

- *Heliotropium* (Heliotrope)
- *Hesperis* (Dame's Violet; Sweet Rocket)
- *Pelargonium* scented-leaved varieties
- *Jasminum* (Jasmine)
- *Matthiola* (Stock)
- *Oenothera fruticosa* (Sundrops)

Plants for Drying

Many plants are suitable for drying. Some can be dried as flowerheads, and others provide interesting and attractive seeding heads or pods.

- *Acanthus mollis* (Bear's Breeches)
- *Achillea filipendulina* (Golden Yarrow)
- *Allium christophii*
- *Anaphalis* (Pearly Everlasting)
- *Astilbe*
- *Astrantia* (Masterwort)
- *Catananche* (Cupid's Dart)
- *Centaurea* (Knapweed)
- *Cortaderia* (Pampas Grass)
- *Echinops* (Globe Thistle)
- *Eryngium* (Sea Holly)
- *Helichrysum*
- *Lavandula* (Lavender)
- *Limonium sinuatum* (*Statice*; Sea Lavender)
- *Lunaria annua* (Honesty)
- *Nigella* (Love-in-a-Mist)
- *Papaver orientale* (Oriental Poppy)
- *Pennisetum* (Feather Grass)
- *Stipa gigantea* (Golden Oats)

Biological controls are relatively expensive and repeat applications may be necessary.

Foliage Plants

Growing plants principally for their attractive foliage is increasingly popular amongst gardeners. These are chosen for their foliage colour or elegant form, and sometimes both.

- *Acanthus mollis* (Bear's Breeches)
- *Aconitum* (Monkshood)
- *Ajuga* (Bugle)
- *Alchemilla* (Lady's Mantle)
- *Artemisia* 'Powis Castle' (Wormwood)
- *Astilbe*
- *Bassia* (*Kochia*; Burning Bush)
- *Calluna* (Ling) requires lime-free soil
- *Cerastium tomentosum* (Snow-in-Summer)
- *Cortaderia* (Pampas Grass)
- *Echeveria*
- *Erica* (Heath) requires lime-free soil, except
        winter-flowering varieties

- *Eryngium* (Sea Holly)
- *Euphorbia* (Spurge)
- *Festuca glauca* 'Elijah Blue' (Blue
        Fescue)
- *Fuchsia magellanica* 'Versicolor'
- *Hedera* (Ivy)
- *Helichrysum*
- *Heuchera*
- *Houttuynia cordata* 'Chameleon'
- *Miscanthus sinensis* 'Zebrinus' (Eulalia Grass)
- *Ophiopogon* (Lily Turf)
- *Ruta* 'Jackman's Blue'(Rue)
- *Stachys byzantina* (Lamb's Ears)
- *Tanacetum parthenium* 'Aureum' (Golden Feverfew)
- *Uncinia rubra* (Red Hook Sedge)

Architectural Plants:

'Architectural' is a term often applied to plants whose main attraction is a stately or striking form. Many that fall into this category are trees or large shrubs, and so outside the range of this book. This selection shows some smaller architectural plants.

- *Acanthus mollis* (Bear's Breeches)
- *Allium christophii*

- *Cordyline* (Cabbage Palm)
- *Cortaderia* (Pampas Grass)
- *Dicksonia* (Tree Fern)
- *Eryngium* (Sea Holly)
- *Euphorbia characias* (Spurge)
- *Gunnera* (Giant Rhubarb)
- *Miscanthus* (Eulalia Grass)
- *Phormium* (New Zealand Flax)
- *Stipa gigantea* (Golden Oat)

Cottage-garden Plants

The traditional cottage garden contains a variety of 'old-fashioned' plants, many grown for their herbal or medicinal properties. This selection contains a range of plants that look the part. Add herbs from the Slug Resistant Herbs listed on page 98 for scent and authenticity.

- *Achillea filipendulina* (Golden Yarrow)
- *Aconitum* (Monkshood)
- *Alchemilla* (Lady's Mantle)
- *Antirrhinum* (Snapdragon)
- *Calendula* (Pot Marigold)
- *Centaurea montana* (Perennial Cornflower)
- *Digitalis* (Foxglove)
- *Geranium* (Cranesbill)
- *Hesperis* (Dame's Violet; Sweet Rocket)
- *Linaria purpurea* (Purple Toadflax)
- *Lobularia* (*Alyssum*; Sweet Alison)
- *Lunaria* (Honesty)
- *Lysimachia* (Loosestrife)
- *Myosotis* (Forget-me-not)
- *Matthiola* (Stock)
- *Nigella* (Love-in-a-Mist)
- *Papaver orientale* (Oriental Poppy)
- *Sedum* 'Autumn Joy' (properly called 'Herbstfreude')
- *Solidago* (Golden Rod)
- *Tanacetum* (Feverfew)
- *Vinca* (Periwinkle)

> Soft bodied slugs and snails generally eat only soft and fleshy plant materials.

Slug Resistant Plants for the Colour-themed Garden

Whether you are planning a whole garden or bed in one colour-range, or are simply looking for a plant of a particular colour, this section will help. Plants are mainly chosen for their flower colour, but a few particularly good foliage plants are included too. See also the section on Foliage Plants, page 88, for further ideas.

Yellow/orange garden

The following have yellow or orange flowers, or have yellow or orange varieties available:

• *Achillea filipendulina* (Golden Yarrow)
• *Alchemilla* (Lady's Mantle)
• *Allium moly* (Golden Garlic)
• *Antirrhinum* (Snapdragon)
• *Aurinia saxatilis* (Golden Alyssum)
• *Calendula* (Pot Marigold)
• *Crocosmia* (Montbretia)
• *Crocus*
• *Eschscholzia* (Californian Poppy)
• *Fuchsia* 'Genii'
• *Gazania* (Treasure Flower)
• *Helianthemum*
• *Limnanthes* (Poached Egg Plant)
• *Lysimachia* (Loosestrife)
• *Phlomis fruticosa* (Jerusalem Sage)
• *Phygelius*
• *Rudbeckia fulgida* (Coneflower)
• *Solidago canadensis* (Golden Rod)
• *Tanacetum parthenium* 'Aureum' (Golden Feverfew)

White garden

It's worth remarking that silver or grey-leaved plants are nearly always slug resistant. The following have white flowers or foliage, or have white varieties available:

• *Aconitum* (Monkshood)
• *Anaphalis* (Pearly Everlasting)

- *Anemone hupehensis* (Japanese Anemone)
- *Antirrhinum* (Snapdragon)
- *Artemisia* 'Powis Castle' (Wormwood)
- *Aster* x *novae-angliae* (Michaelmas Daisy)
- *Astrantia* (Masterwort)
- *Calluna* (Ling). Needs lime-free soil
- *Catananche* (Cupid's Dart)
- *Centaurea montana* (Perennial Cornflower)
- *Cerastium tomentosum* (Snow-in-Summer)
- *Crocus*
- *Digitalis* (Foxglove)
- *Erica* (Heath) lime-free soil required, except winter-flowering varieties
- *Erigeron karvinskianus* (Mexican Daisy)
- *Gaura*
- *Geranium* (Cranesbill)
- *Lobularia* (*Alyssum*; Sweet Alison)
- *Malva moschata* (Musk Mallow)
- *Osteospermum* (Cape Daisy)
- *Paeonia* (Peony)
- *Sidalcea* (Prairie Mallow)
- *Tanacetum parthenium* (Feverfew)

Blue/purple garden

Blue is an unusual colour in the garden, however the do provide a subtle contrast with green. The following have blue or purple flowers or foliage, or have blue or purple varieties available.

- *Aconitum* (Monkshood)
- *Ajuga* (Bugle)
- *Aster amellus*
- *Aster* x *novae-angliae* (Michaelmas Daisy)
- *Borago* (Borage)
- *Campanula poscharskyana* (Serbian Bellflower)
- *Catananche* (Cupid's Dart)
- *Centaurea montana* (Perennial Cornflower)
- *Chionodoxa* (Glory of the Snows)
- *Crocus*
- *Digitalis* (Foxglove)
- *Eryngium* (Sea Holly)
- *Festuca* 'Elijah Blue' (Blue Fescue)

Garden Plants that Slugs Won't Eat!

- *Geranium* (Cranesbill)
- *Linaria purpurea* (Purple Toadflax)
- *Monarda* (Bergamot; Bee Balm)
- *Muscari* (Grape Hyacinth)
- *Myosotis* (Forgetmenot)
- *Nepeta* x *faasenii* (Catmint)
- *Nigella* (Love-in-a-Mist)
- *Perovskia* (Russian Sage)
- *Polemonium foliosissimum* (Jacob's Ladder)
- *Rosmarinus* (Rosemary)
- *Salvia* x *superba*
- *Scilla* (Squill)
- *Triteleia*
- *Verbena bonariensis* (Tall Vervain)
- *Veronica spicata* (Spiked Speedwell)

Red/pink garden
The following have red or pink flowers or foliage, or have red or pink varieties available:

- *Allium christophii*
- *Anemone hupehensis* (Japanese Anemone)
- *Antirrhinum* (Snapdragon)
- *Armeria* (Thrift)
- *Aster amellus*
- *Aster* x *frikartii*
- *Aster* x *novae-angliae* (Michaelmas Daisy)
- *Astrantia* (Masterwort)
- *Calluna* (Ling) Requires lime-free soil
- *Centaurea montana* (Perennial Cornflower)
- *Centaurea dealbata*
- *Crocosmia* 'Lucifer'
- *Dianthus deltoides* (Maiden Pink)
- *Dierama* (Angel's Fishing Rods)
- *Digitalis* (Foxglove)
- *Erica* (Heath) requires lime-free soil, except winter-flowering varieties
- *Malva moschata* (Musk Mallow)
- *Gazania* (Treasure Flower)
- *Geranium* (Cranesbill)

Many people use six times the amount of slug pellets actually required. One pellet every 3-4 inches (8-10 cm), all around the plant, is just as effective.

- *Osteospermum* (Cape Daisy)
- *Geum* (Avens)
- *Helianthemum*
- *Monarda* (Bergamot; Bee Balm)
- *Paeonia* (Peony)
- *Papaver orientale* (Oriental Poppy)
- *Phygelius* (Cape Fuchsia)
- *Sedum* 'Autumn Joy' properly called 'Herbstfreude'

* *Sidalcea* (Prairie Mallow)
* *Uncinia rubra* (Red Hook Sedge)

Late Summer and Autumn Flowering Slug Resistant Plants

Plants that flower late in the season are particularly valuable since they give the garden a boost when many other plants are past their best. Extend your garden's season with some of these.

- *Achillea filipendulina* (Golden Yarrow)
- *Aconitum* (Monkshood)
- *Anaphalis* (Pearly Everlasting)
- *Anemone hupehensis* (Japanese Anemone)
- *Aster amellus*
- *Aster* x *frikartii*
- *Aster* x *novae-angliae* (Michaelmas Daisy)
- *Astilbe*
- *Calluna* (Ling) requires lime-free soil
- *Centaurea dealbata* (Perennial Cornflower)
- *Crocosmia* (Montbretia)
- *Erica* (Heath) requires lime-free soil
- *Eryngium* (Sea Holly)
- *Galtonia* (Summer Hyacinth)
- *Rudbeckia fulgida* (Coneflower)
- *Sedum* 'Autumn Joy' ('Herbstfreude')
- *Solidago canadensis* (Golden Rod)

Early Flowering Slug Resistant Plants

Early-flowering plants are specially dear to the gardener's heart - and appear just when the slugs are getting into their stride. This selection will help to avert any early-season heartbreak.

- *Aurinia* (Golden Alyssum)
- *Chionodoxa* (Glory of the Snows)
- *Crocus*
- *Erica* (Heath) winter-flowering varieties
- *Euphorbia myrsinites* (Spurge)
- *Hyacinthoides* (Bluebell)
- *Muscari* (Grape Hyacinth)
- *Myosotis* (Forgetmenot)
- *Rosmarinus* (Rosemary)
- *Scilla* (Squill)

Dusty substances such as ash from a wood burning stove will help to deter slugs and snails, provided they form a complete boundary around the plant. This remedy is only temporary, however, as it needs to be renewed after rainfall.

Drought Resistant Plants

Alstroemeria (Peruvian Lily) - Orange variety rampages - there are others. Need sun. Very attractive to slugs and snails.

Golden *Alyssum* (*Aurinia*) - A good edging plant.

Antirrhinum (Snapdragon)

Begonia - Not all varieties need deadheading. Slugs and snails seem unattracted to these popular bedding plants.

Bellis (Daisy)

Calendula (Pot Marigold) - Pot marigolds are recommended as slug and snail resistant.

Centaurea dealbata (Pink Perennial Cornflower/Knapweed)

Centaurea montana (Perennial Cornflower/Knapweed) - White variety are both slug and snail resistant.

Clarkia (*Godetia*)

Dianthus deltoides (Pinks)

Eschscholzia (Californian Poppy)

Fuschia

Gaillardia - Resembles small sunflowers.

Gazania (Treasure Flower)

Geranium

Geum - Flowers all summer.

Helenium -Middle border height - Summer and autumn daisies usually yellow.

Helianthemum

Helichrysum - Front of border plant.

Heliotropium (Cherry Pie) - Middle border height - blues, purple and pink colours usually. likes sun.

Hyacinth - Summer flowering bulbs, usually white. Also known as Galtonia candicans.- slug and snail resistant.

Garden Plants that Slugs Won't Eat!

Herbs - Like it dry - slugs rarely eat them - some have flowers e.g. Borage has a pretty sparkling blue flower, whilst coriander has a small white dusting of blossom.

Lavendula (Lavender)

Limnanthes (Poached Egg Plant) Edging plant.

Limonium sinuatum (Sea Lavender; Statice) - Slug and draught tolerant, will die back into a rosette in the winter, then grow in spring and flowers again. Limonium generally grows best on poor, free-draining soil in full sun.

Lobularia (Alyssum; Sweet Alison)

Lunaria (Honesty)

Lysimachia - Front of border plant needs sun or semi-shade.

Malcolmia (Virginia Stock)

Marjoram (herb) - Evergreen that likes it dry, spreads and is good for trailing over baskets, tubs and edgings.

Matthiola (Stock)

Mesembryanthemum (Livingstone Daisy)

Mimulus - Likes sun and dappled shade but a bit of damp.

Mirabilis jalapa - Looks like ***Nicotiana*** (tobacco plants).

Monarda (Bergamot) Middle border plant - likes sun and a little moisture.

Myosotis (Forgetmenot) - Quick spreading plant - slug and snail resistant.

Nigella (Love-in-a-Mist)

Osteospermum (Cape Daisy)

Papaver nudicaule (Iceland Poppy)

Pelargonium - Scented-leaved varieties - slug and snail resistant.

Phygelius - Middle or back of border plant. Spreading habit.

Rudbeckia fulgida (Coneflower)

Senecio leucostachys - Grey foliage plant that likes a drysoil.

Stocks - dependent on variety - slug and snail resistant.

Valerian, Red (Centranthus) - spreads a little - flowers all summer. Needs sun - slug and snail resistant.

Verbena

Slugs in the compost bin may be beneficial because they consume waste material which is then converted into humus. However, the slugs will inevitably be breeding in your heap and so by spreading the compost around your garden you will also be distributing adults as well as their eggs. They can be controlled by watering the heap with a dilute solution of Slug Clear liquid. The more creatures and micro-organisms devouring the waste the quicker it will break down into useable organic matter and you may feel that this is more worthwhile.

Popular Herbs

Herbs are generally slug and snail resistant and valuable garden plants for their scent, flowers and usefulness in kitchen and medicinal properties. Some herbs have all three benefits and many are used in pot-pourri.

Allium schoenoprasum (Chives) - Ornamental; edible leaves.

Borago (Borage) - Decorative; edible flowers.

Chamemelum and *Anthemis* (Camomiles) - scented.

Coriandrum (Coriander) - attractive, edible leaves and seeds; aromatic; culinary; medicinal.

Foeniculum (Fennel) - Graceful; aromatic, edible leaves and roots; medicinal properties.

Laurus nobilis (Bay) - Decorative shrub, with scented leaves; culinary; medicinal.

Marjoram - Evergreen, likes it dry, spreads and is good for edgings. Used in everyday cooking and medicinal.

Melissa (Lemon Balm) - Scented; edible leaves.

Mentha (Mint) - Decorative; scented; edible leaves.

Ocimum (Basil) - Scented; edible leaves.

Origanum (Marjoram) Decorative; scented, edible leaves.

Rosmarinus (Rosemary) - Decorative; scented; edible leaves; culinary; medicinal.

Salvia officinalis (Sage) - has so many uses. It is Aromatic; scented; has edible leave for use in cooking, is medicinal and used in most remedies for its essential oils. As a garden plant it is green all year and looks lovely trailing over brick paths.

Symphytum (Comfrey) - Decorative; medicinal, often used as a fertilizer, mulch and compost activator.

Thymus (Thyme) - Decorative; scented; edible leaves.

Around £114 million is spent every year on garden chemicals, a great many of which are slug control preparations. Although organic products are included within this, they are claimed to only represent a tiny proportion of the total figure and it is now quite fashionable to produce your own methods of slug control, i.e. garlic wash, salt baths, upturned grapefruit baths and beer traps.

Alternative Planting Suggestions

What should I plant instead?

Finally given up on the delphiniums? But what could you plant instead that will fill a similar height and space in the garden? There are few exact matches for each plant in terms of colour, season and size, but here are a few ideas for replacements for your slug-susceptible plants.

Aubrietas. If your aubrietas have been bitten to pieces, try another spring-flowering, trailing rockplant, the Serbian bellflower **C*ampanula poscharskyana*.** It forms mounds of evergreen foliage and has spikes of bright purple-blue flowers.

Colchicums. These are easy enough to replace: try autumn-flowering crocus, instead.

Coneflowers (*Echinacea*). The late summer-flowering daisy **Aster x *frikartii*** would seem your best bet if your echinaceas have been decimated. It is available in similar colours, and is a strong-growing, disease-resistant plant.

Delphiniums. Tall blue plants are a little thin on the ground, but monkshood (*Aconitum*) looks very similar, though it does require a little shade. Or forget it and try growing foxgloves **(*Digitalis*)** instead. There are lots of lovely colours available, but sadly not blue.

French or African marigolds (*Tagetes*). **Pot marigolds (*Calendula*)** - are the nearest match, as cheerful yellow and orange annuals.

Heleniums. Try growing the very similar-looking **Rudbeckia** or **Gaillardia** instead.

Hostas. Nothing beats the cool beauty of hosta foliage. But what a mess it looks full of holes. There are lots of other lovely foliage plants to choose from. See page 88.

Hyacinths. Forget outdoor hyacinths and grow **muscari** or **bluebells.** Grow the hyacinths indoors where you can more easily appreciate the scent.

Lobelias. Annual lobelias eaten again? Why not try lesser Periwinkles *(Vinca minor).* They come in similar flower colours, trail fetchingly over the sides of containers, and are perennnial, so they'll last for years.

Lupins (*Lupinus*). Nothing else looks quite like a lupin, but if yours are slug-bitten consider **Foxgloves** instead. They are not disimilar in shape and come in much the same colour range, including yellows and apricots.

Morning Glories (*Ipomoea*). An interesting substitute for morning glories is the cup-and-saucer vine *(Cobaea scandens)*. It doesn't have quite the colour range, but it is a fast-growing annual that will enjoy a similar sunny spot.

Nerines. If you like the sugary-pink flowers of nerines you could try *Schizostylis*, which looks very similar and is rather less slug-susceptible. Or forget it and grow crocosmias for late season colour.

Phlox. If your taller phlox are bitten to pieces time after time, try growing sweet rocket *(Hesperis matronalis)*. It's not so glamorous as phlox, but it does have an excellent scent and will occupy a similar space in the border.

Red-hot Pokers (*Kniphofia*). These unmistakable plants are tricky to replace, if you're having problems. If it's the flower-spikes you like, then perhaps the cape fuchsia *(Phygelius)* might help. They are available in strong shades of red and yellow. If it's the handsome grassy leaves that appeal, then a New Zealand flax *(Phormium)* could be the answer. Available in reds, greens and novelty stripes.

There is a new hosta called 'Sun & Substance' that offers some resistance to snail and slug attack.

Salvias. Scarlet salvias for summer bedding can make a stunning display - unless the slugs get to them. If your soil is not too dry, similar colouring can be provided by varieties of mimulus. In a dry, sunny garden try the rock rose **(*Helianthemum*)**. These not only come in a stunning range of colours, including bright scarlet, they are also evergreen and perennial, so they'll still be there in future years.

Sunflowers (*Helianthus*). There's no easy substitute for the tall sunflowers, but if you like the smaller, more compact varieties, *Gaillardia* or *Rudbeckia* are a reasonable replacement.

Sweet peas (*Lathyrus odoratus*). The fabulous scent of sweet peas is well-nigh irreplaceable. Everlasting peas are more slug-resistant and generally look similar, but without the scent. If you must have scent, forget the peas and grow honeysuckle or jasmine instead.

Sweet Williams (*Dianthus barbatus*). Forget sweet Williams if the slugs get them. Just plant **perennial pinks** instead. There is quite a choice of 'cottage garden pinks', all in similar colour

ranges to sweet williams, and beautifully scented. They have lovely silver-grey foliage, too. Problem solved.

Tobacco Plants (*Nicotiana*). Trouble with your tobacco plants? Try the **Marvel of Peru (*Mirabilis jalapa*)** instead. It looks reasonably similar, comes in an excellent range of colours and is nicely scented.

Chickens supplement their diet with slugs, snails, grubs and bits of greenery that they find for themselves together with plenty of insects they scratch up from within their run.
Useful if you have the space for one or two hens.

More Facts About Slugs and Snails

Slugs and snails are able to sense food from two metres away.

Encourage future young gardeners by collecting slugs and snails at night with a torch. The excitement of a late night, coupled with catching the creatures, will encourage the children into the garden. Turn it into a treasure hunt by offering a prize for whoever catches the most.

Tadpoles will develop into frogs and frogs will help keep your garden free of slugs! A great reason to invest in a small pond.

Eelworms are a good biological control method of slug and snail control Whilst successful, ensure soil temperature and the moisture content is at the correct level. The method also needs repeating every six weeks and is expensive.

It would be useful to gardeners if garden centres put a warning sticker on plants that are prone to slug and snail attack. This knowledge would allow the buyer to put down a few slug pellets immediately they planted their new plants.

Slug pellets were in the top ten best-seller listing in a poll conducted by a leading market research company. It is interesting to note that although there has been a steady rise in organic products to control slugs and snails, organic killers are lagging behind at number 32.

Hand-picking slugs and snails at dusk is a recommended method of control. Try regular night-time or dusk forays, armed with a bucket and a torch. What do you do with them then? Well, disposal methods are up to you! We add a tablespoon of salt to the bucket of water. Cruel, yes, but highly effective!

Hedgehogs are renowned for devouring slugs voraciously. They have no fear of ponds and are actually good swimmers if they happen to fall in but it is essential that they have a means of escape from the water. A hedgehog can cover half a mile in one night - that's meeting up with a lot of slugs! However these prickly garden friends are getting less and less so it is time to try other methods of removing slugs and snails from your garden.

Runner beans being eaten by slugs? The easiest way is to pick them off at dusk and early morning saunters into the garden can alleviate a lot of the problems, particularly after a shower.

Don't forget to look in disused flowerpots - many slugs and snails linger there, ready for picking and disposing easily.

100 Plants that Slugs & Snails *will* attack

Quick Reference List

All these plants are said to be susceptible to slug or snail damage. Think twice before planting them if you have a slug problem in your garden. Their susceptibility varies, so for fuller information see our Directory of Plants, (*See page 25*).

Adonis (Pheasant's Eye)
Alstroemeria (Peruvian Lily)
Amaryllis (Jersey Lily)
Amicia
Anacyclus (Mount Atlas Daisy)
Anagallis (Pimpernel)
Anemone, except *A. hupehensis, A. hybrida*
Anemonopsis
Anethum (Dill)
Anthyllis
Arctotis (African Daisy)
Asarina (Creeping Snapdragon)
Asarum (Wild Ginger)
Auricula
Bidens
Brugmansia (Angel's Trumpet)
Calceolaria (Slipper Flower)
Campanula, except *C. poscharskyana*
Cardamine
Cardiocrinum
Chaerophyllum (Chervil)
Clintonia
Codonopsis
Colchicum (Autumn Crocus)
Consolida (Larkspur)
Coreopsis (Tickseed)
Crambe
Cyananthus
Dahlia
Darmera (Umbrella Plant)

Delphinium
Deutzia
Dianthus barbatus (Sweet William)
Disporum (Fairy Bells)
Dodecatheon (Shooting Star)
Draba
Echinacea (Cone Flower)
Edraianthus
Epimedium
Eriophyllum
Erythronium (Dog's Tooth Violet)
Fritillaria (Fritillary)
Gentiana (Gentian)
Gerbera
Glaucidium
Gypsophila (perennials only)
Haberlea
Helenium (Sneezeweed)
Helianthus (Sunflower)
Hepatica
Hosta (Plantain Lily)
Houstonia
Hyacinthus (Hyacinth)
Hylomecon
Hypsela
Iberis amara (Annual Candytuft)
Ionopsidium
Ipomoea (Morning Glory)
Ixia (Corn Lily)
Kirengeshoma
Kniphofia (Red Hot Poker)
Lathyrus odoratus (Sweet Pea)
Leontopodium (Edelweiss)
Ligularia
Lilium, except *Lilium regale*
Liriope
Lobelia
Lupinus (Lupin)
Lychnis except *Lychnis coronaria*
Maianthemum (May Lily)
Marrow and courgette

Garden Plants that Slugs Won't Eat!

Myrrhis (Sweet Cicely)
Narcissus (Daffodil)
Nerine
Nicotiana (Tobacco Flower)
Nierembergia (Cup Flower)
Nomocharis
Oenanthe (Water Dropwort)
Omphalodes, especially *Omphalodes luciliae*
Onopordum (Scotch Thistle)
Ourisia
Oxalis
Papaver, except *Papaver nudicaule* and *Papaver orientale*
Paradisia
Paris
Peas
Phlox adsurgens
Phlox divaricata
Phlox stolonifera
Physoplexis
Pinguicula (Butterwort)
Platycodon (Balloon Flower)
Pleione (Outdoor Orchid)
Potato
Pratia
Ramonda
Rhododendron
Roscoea

Salvia (scarlet bedding salvias)
Saxifraga cochlearis (Silver Saxifrage)
Senecio
Silybum (Milk Thistle)
Soldanella
Spinach
Stokesia (Stokes' Aster)
Strawberry
Symphyandra
Tagetes (French and African Marigolds)
Tithonia (Mexican Sunflower)
Tricyrtis (Toad Lily)
Trillium (Wood Lily)
Uvularia (Bellwort)